Just Joking

Stories for Listening and Discussion

Sandra Heyer

Just Joking: Stories for Listening and Discussion

Pearson Education, 10 Bank Street, White Plains, NY 10606

Executive editor: Laura Le Dréan
Associate acquisitions editor: Amy McCormick
Development editor: Dana Klinek
Production editor: Laurie Neaman
Production coordinator: Melissa Leyva
Director of manufacturing: Patrice Fraccio
Senior manufacturing buyer: Dave Dickey
Cover design: Judy Allen
Text design: Ann France
Associate paging manager: Paula D. Williams
Text font: Palatino 10/11
Illustrations: Mike Erickson

Photo credits: cover, middle row, far right Andrew McCaul/Image Bank. **Page 7**, © Fotosearch. **Page 12**, © Fotosearch; **bottom left**, © Bonnie Kamin/Photo Edit. **Page 24**, © Douglas Healey/ The New York Times. **Page 37**, © Taxi/ Getty Images. **Page 43**, © Fotosearch. **Page 73**, © Charles Ofria/ www.familycar.com. **Page 91**, © David Rubinger/Getty Images.

Text credits: **Page 7**, The idea is from *Zero Prep*, by Laurel Pollard and Natalie Hess, Alta Book Center Publishers, 1997 ("Gift Exchange," p. 75). **Page 8**, The joke was contributed by Francisco Dominguez. **Page 30**, The drawing and sentences are by Angel Zeferino. This type of discussion activity is suggested by Sharron Bassano and Mary Ann Christison in *Drawing Out*, Alta Book Center Publishers, 1995. **Page 54**, The writing example is by Ana L. Rangel. **Page 72**, The questions were taken from a survey conducted in November and December of 2000 and January of 2001 on the Web site www.conversely.com. **Page 102**, The map and descriptions are by Rosa Ariuntsetseg. **Page 113**, The memory tips in the Answer Key are drawn from "25 Tips to Recharge Your Memory" by Rick Chillot, *Prevention*, February 1999.

Library of Congress Cataloging-in-Publication Data

Heyer, Sandra.
   Just joking: stories for listening and discussion/by Sandra Heyer.
      p. cm.
ISBN 0-13-193022-2
   1. English language—Textbooks for foreign speakers. 2. Discussion–Problems exercises, etc. 3. Listening–Problems, exercises, etc. 4. Readers. I. Title

PE1128.H4357 2005
428.3'4–dc22

2004027106

LONGMAN ON THE **WEB**

Longman.com offers online resources for teachers and students. Access our Companion Websites, our online catalog, and our local offices around the world.

Visit us at **longman.com**.

Printed in the United States of America
2 3 4 5 6 7 8 9 10—BAH—09 08 07 06 05

Dedication

For my dad, whose puns are pretty good . . . most of the time

Contents

To The Teacher

Just Joking is a listening and discussion text for high-beginning learners of English. As the title suggests, each unit is centered on a joke—a humorous, illustrated story that concludes with a punch line. The jokes are suitable for adolescents, young adults, and adults. *Just Joking* is ideal in a listening/speaking course but it can be used in any class to motivate and relax learners and to add variety to the lessons.

The stories in *Just Joking* have been carefully selected and field-tested for their universal appeal; that is, they are jokes that almost anyone, almost anywhere in the world would find funny. However, you might find that people from different cultures, and even from subcultures within those cultures, respond differently to these jokes. That would not be surprising. Research in humor, most notably a 2001 study sponsored by the British Association for the Advancement of Science, has established that there are national preferences for certain types of jokes. Nevertheless, this study also indicated that while people might prefer one joke over another, some jokes are universally popular. These jokes have several characteristics in common. First, they are moderate in length—an average of slightly over 100 words. Second, they share the same rhetorical form—they are stories with an unexpected ending. The study bore out preferences that learners who field-tested *Just Joking* had already expressed. The jokes that were chosen for this book—many of which were field-tested long before the 2001 study—have an average length of 114 words, and all have a surprise ending.

Each unit in *Just Joking* is comprised of six sections. Following are explanations of the purpose of each section and suggestions for using it.

1. BEFORE LISTENING

This section gives students a preview of the story's vocabulary and content.

A. The first exercise in this section targets words students need to know in order to understand the story. The answers to most of these exercises are in the Answer Key.

B. The second exercise invites students to speculate on the story's content. There is a single picture that prompts a single question. To emphasize that any logical guess at the answer is acceptable, you might ask students to respond orally, informally volunteering possible answers.

2. LISTENING TO THE STORY

Students listen to the story as the CD plays it or as you read it aloud. They look at the pictures as they listen. If you choose to read the story, you will find the story script in the back of the book. Begin by saying "Number One," and read the part of the story the first picture illustrates. Students look at the picture and listen. Then say "Number Two" and read the corresponding part of the story while students look at the second picture and listen. Continue reading the story in this manner. Saying the numbers of the pictures as you tell the story ensures that all eyes are on the same picture. Feel free to supplement the story script with lines of your own if you think they enhance comprehension. Also feel free to act out parts of the story. In Unit 13, for example, you could demonstrate actions like "put in reverse," "back up," and "crash."

3. CHECKING YOUR UNDERSTANDING

A. For the first exercise, students hear the story again as the CD plays it or as you read it aloud. This time, however, students complete a task as they listen: They fill in words, circle words, cross out wrong words, or complete sentences. Whereas the previous section gives students a global understanding of the story, this section draws students' attention to details. The answers to this exercise are in the Answer Key.

B. The second exercise is an oral partner exercise. After students fill in the missing words and check their answers in the Answer Key, you may wish to read the sentences aloud, asking students to repeat after you, to model pronunciation and intonation. Students then read this section aloud with a partner.

4. LISTENING AND WRITING

This is a dictation exercise. The sentences for dictation constitute a summary of the story. Students listen to either the recording or to you reading the sentences. If you choose to read the sentences, a suggested method is to read each sentence three times. First, read the sentence at normal speed. Then read the sentence again, this time breaking it into chunks of meaning. ("They were afraid...his parachute . . . wouldn't open.") Finally, read the sentence again at normal speed.

The direction line tells students to cover the sentences with a piece of paper and then lift the paper after they are finished writing to check their work. Students who find writing challenging, however, might want to leave the sentences uncovered so they can check their work as they write. If you would like to give students this option, a discreet way to offer it is to say, "If writing English is easy for you, cover the sentences. If writing English is not easy for you, don't cover the sentences. Look at each sentence and then write it down." Students with only basic literacy skills in English will find copying the sentences challenging enough. If, on the other hand, you wish to make the dictation exercise more challenging, you might want to try the following variations:

The Walking Dictation. Students place their books on the opposite side of the room, open to the LISTENING AND WRITING page. They read the first sentence, memorize it, walk back to their desks, and write the sentence on their own paper. They continue walking back and forth from their desks to their books until they have written all the sentences on their own paper. They then retrieve their books to check their work. The "walking dictation" can also be done as a partner exercise, with one student walking over to the book, memorizing a sentence, and dictating it to a partner, who writes it. In each case, the walking student goes to the book and "carries" back one sentence at a time.

The Disappearing Dictation. Write the sentences on the board. Read the first sentence aloud. Students repeat in unison. Erase two or three words in the sentence, randomly choosing words to erase. (For example, "A rich woman _____ her mother a _____.") Say the entire sentence again (including the words that have been erased); students repeat in chorus. (You may wish to point at individual words as students repeat the sentence, pointing even to the words that have disappeared.) Continue erasing words two or three at a time, saying the sentence, and asking students to repeat, until finally the whole sentence is erased. Students then write the "disappeared" sentence from memory. Repeat the process with the remaining sentences.

5. RETELLING THE STORY

A. In the first exercise, students write the story in their own words, using the keywords as prompts. (All verbs in this section are given in their unconjugated form; students will need to decide whether they wish to retell the story in the present or past tense. Either form is natural in joke-telling.) This can be a homework assignment. You may also wish to try these in-class writing activities:

Group Writing. Students tell the story to you, calling out contributions, and you write the students' sentences on the board. Tell the students not to be too concerned about correctness; the idea here is to get the story up on the board quickly. After you have recorded the students' sentences, read each sentence aloud and ask students to correct any errors. (You may need to underline errors if students cannot identify them.)

Dictacomp. Read the script of the story aloud to the students twice, first slowly and then at normal speed. When you are finished reading the story, students write it from memory, trying to write it exactly as they heard it. Students open their books and check their writing against the original. This activity is called a dictacomp because it has elements of both a dictation and a composition. A variation of the dictacomp is the Miming Dictacomp. Begin by reading the story twice, as above, but then act out scenes from the story. Your movements are prompts for students' writing. The Miming Dictacomp works well for stories with plenty of action, like "The Parking Space."

B. In the second exercise, students retell the story to a partner. This activity works best if the partner has not heard the story before. If you have the help of a volunteer or classroom aide, you can divide the class into two groups of equal numbers and separate the groups. With the help of the teacher and the activities in the text, students in Group One prepare to tell a joke from one unit while students in Group Two, directed by the aide or volunteer, prepare to tell a joke from a different unit. Then Groups One and Two meet. Students from Group One find partners from Group Two and tell their partners the "Group One joke." Students from Group Two tell their partners the "Group Two joke." Both teller and listener refer to the LISTENING TO THE STORY page as the joke is told.

If another class (at the same level or at a higher proficiency level) meets at the same time, you might "borrow" the students from that class for ten minutes. Students find a partner among the "borrowed" students, and, with the help of the LISTENING TO THE STORY page, tell the story to their partners.

A contest can encourage students to tell the story outside of class. Students get the signatures of all the people to whom they tell the story (in English!). The student who brings the most signatures back to class the next day wins a small prize.

This simple activity—telling the joke to a partner—can give students' self-confidence an enormous boost. Perhaps no aspect of learning a language is more demoralizing than the realization that the learner lacks the language skills to (intentionally) make people laugh. If you look around the room after your students have told the joke to a partner, you will notice that it is difficult to discern from the expressions on people's faces who told the joke and who heard it; both teller and listener will be smiling. Perhaps the tellers are smiling not just because the joke is funny but because they have had the satisfaction of making someone laugh.

6. TALKING ABOUT THE TOPIC

Each unit ends with a spin-off activity that gets students talking about the topic of the joke. Most of the activities require that students first put their thoughts in writing, either by answering questions or completing statements. Giving students time to collect their thoughts and write them down makes them more inclined to speak; this is especially true for students who are concerned about speaking correctly. You might find that conversation flows easily. Laughter can be an anxiety reducer and a social unifier, so a funny story often eases the way to a relaxed and amiable discussion. In addition, a joke's humor often derives from exaggerating human foibles and fears, which makes it easier to share our own more modest shortcomings. We may be forgetful at times, but we are not as forgetful as the woman who forgot she had a memory problem, and although we may have given a gift that was not appreciated, at least it was not a fifty-thousand-dollar bird!

The purpose of *Just Joking* is to improve your students' listening and speaking skills while decreasing their anxiety and increasing their self-confidence. Above all, it is hoped that the stories in *Just Joking* fill your classroom with laughter.

Acknowledgments

I wish to thank:

- my congenial colleagues Anjie Martin, Marge Fischer, and Katherine Conover, who opened their classrooms to me so that I could field test jokes and activities;

- the learners in the Whitewater, Wisconsin, Community Education ESL Program, who responded enthusiastically to the jokes that were included in this text and who tolerated politely those that were not; and

- illustrator Mike Erickson, whose drawings and phone messages made me laugh.

Sandra Heyer

The Birthday Present

❶ BEFORE LISTENING

A. Complete the sentences with the words below. Write your answer on the line. (The first one is done for you.)

languages   pet   shop   delicious   send   rich

1. If you have ten million dollars, you are _____ *rich* _____.

2. An animal that lives in your house (a dog, cat, bird, or fish, for example) is a

   _____.

3. Your brother lives in another country. It is his birthday, so you

   _____ him a present.

4. You can buy things at a _____. (It is usually smaller than

   a store.)

5. If you speak Spanish and English, you speak two _____.

6. Food that tastes very good is _____.

B. You are going to hear a story about a woman who wanted to buy a present for her mother. Look at the picture. Where did the woman go?

LISTENING TO THE STORY

Look at the pictures as you listen to the story.

❸ CHECKING YOUR UNDERSTANDING

🎧 **A. Listen to the story again. As you listen, circle the correct word.**

1. A rich woman was ((thinking) / talking) about her mother.

2. She wanted to (make / send) her mother a nice birthday present.

3. The woman went to a (flower / pet) shop.

4. She saw a beautiful (bird / fish).

5. The bird could sing, and it could speak (six / seven) languages.

6. It cost (five / fifty) thousand dollars.

7. The next day the woman (called / e-mailed) her mother.

8. Her mother said, "I'm eating it right now. It's (expensive / delicious)."

B. Write the missing word on the line. Check your answers in the Answer Key. Then sit with a partner and read the conversation aloud. Student A begins.

A	B

A

1. May I help you?

2. How about this _____?

3. It can sing, and it can

   _____ seven languages.

4. It's fifty _____

   dollars.

5. Sure, we can send it.

B

Yes, I'm looking for a birthday

_____**present**_____ for my mother.

Maybe. What can it do?

How much is it?

I'll take it. Can you _____

it to my mother?

That's great. Her birthday is tomorrow.

❹ LISTENING AND WRITING

🎧 **Cover the sentences below with a piece of paper. You will hear the sentences. As you listen, write them on the lines. Then lift your paper and check your writing.**

1. A rich woman sent her mother a bird.

2. The bird could sing.

3. It could speak seven languages.

4. It cost fifty thousand dollars.

5. The woman's mother didn't know the bird was expensive.

6. She ate it for dinner.

1. _____

2. _____

3. _____

4. _____

5. _____

6. _____

❺ RETELLING THE STORY

A. Write the story in your own words on the lines. Use the keywords to help you.

- rich woman, think, mother

- want, send, birthday present

- go, pet shop

- see, beautiful bird

- bird, sing, speak, languages

- cost, fifty thousand dollars

- buy, bird

- send, bird, mother

- next day, call, telephone

- ask, like, bird

- eat now

- delicious

_____

_____

_____

_____

_____

_____

_____

_____

_____

_____

_____

_____

_____

_____

**B. Tell the story to a partner. Use the pictures on the LISTENING TO THE STORY
   page to help you.**

❻ TALKING ABOUT THE TOPIC

What Is a Great Present?

Exchange "presents" with the people in your class.

- With the class, make a list of presents people like to give and receive. Your teacher will write your list on the board.

- Write your name on a small piece of paper. Put the piece of paper in a box. Your classmates will put their pieces of paper in the box, too. Then reach into the box and take a piece of paper. You are going to give that person a "present."

- Choose a "present" from the list on the board. Then copy this letter on your own paper.

Dear _____ ,

I want to give you _____ for a present

because _____ .

Your friend,

_____

- Complete the letter as you copy it. For example:

Dear Anna,

I want to give you a music CD for a present because I know you like music.

Your friend,

Radu

- Fold your letter and deliver it to your classmate.

- After you open your "present," tell the class what you received. Tell the class why you like your "present."

❶ BEFORE LISTENING

A. Look at the photo. You are going to hear a story about a man who wanted to try this sport. Which words do you think will be in the story? Circle five words. (The first one is done for you.)

skydiving

umbrella

swimming

exciting

dangerous

parachute

hungry

ball

worried

B. When the man told his friends he wanted to try skydiving, they were worried. Look at the picture. What do you think his friends were worried about?

🎧 Look at the pictures as you listen to the story.

❸ CHECKING YOUR UNDERSTANDING

🎧 **A. Listen to the story again. As you listen, complete the sentences. Circle the letter of your answer.**

1. A young man wanted to try an
   - (a.) exciting sport.
   - b. interesting sport.

2. He decided to try
   - a. bicycling.
   - b. skydiving.

3. He went to a store and bought
   - a. an airplane.
   - b. a parachute.

4. "I'm going to try skydiving!" he told his
   - a. friends.
   - b. parents.

5. His friends were
   - a. worried.
   - b. happy.

6. They said, "Skydiving is
   - a. expensive."
   - b. dangerous."

7. They asked, "What will you do if your parachute doesn't
   - a. open?"
   - b. close?"

8. The young man said, "I'll take it back to the store and ask for
   - a. a new parachute."
   - b. my money back."

B. Write the missing word on the line. Check your answers in the Answer Key. Then sit with a partner and read the conversation aloud. Student A begins.

A	B
1. Hi! What's new?	I'm going to ___try___ skydiving.
2. Are you sure you want to do that?	Yes. I think it will be _____.
3. Isn't it _____?	Not really. Remember: I'll have a _____.
4. Yes. But what will you do if your parachute doesn't _____?	I'll take it _____ to the store and ask for my money back.

④ LISTENING AND WRITING

Cover the sentences below with a piece of paper. You will hear the sentences. As you listen, write them on the lines. Then lift your paper and check your writing.

1. A young man wanted to try skydiving.

2. He bought a parachute.

3. His friends were worried.

4. They thought skydiving was dangerous.

5. They were afraid his parachute wouldn't open.

6. The young man wasn't worried.

7. If his parachute didn't open, he would get his money back.

1. _____

2. _____

3. _____

4. _____

5. _____

6. _____

7. _____

⑤ RETELLING THE STORY

A. Write the story in your own words on the lines. Use the keywords to help you.

- young man, try, exciting sport
- decide, try, skydiving
- buy, parachute
- friends, worried
- skydiving, dangerous
- what, do, parachute, open
- take back, store, ask, money, back

_____

_____

_____

_____

_____

_____

_____

_____

_____

_____

_____

_____

_____

B. Tell the story to a partner. Use the pictures on the LISTENING TO THE STORY page to help you.

❻ TALKING ABOUT THE TOPIC

Do You Like Exciting Sports?

A. Would you like to try these exciting sports?

skydiving

snowboarding

white-water rafting

rock climbing

Circle *want* or *don't want*. Then complete the sentences. Share your answers with the class. For example:

I (want /(don't want)) to try skydiving because ___ *it is expensive* ___.

1. I (want / don't want) to try skydiving because _____.

2. I (want / don't want) to try snowboarding because _____.

3. I (want / don't want) to try white-water rafting because _____.

4. I (want / don't want) to try rock climbing because _____.

B. What are other exciting (or not-so-exciting) sports you'd like to try? Tell the class.

The Memory Problem

❶ BEFORE LISTENING

A. When people can't remember things, we say they have a memory problem. Do you have trouble remembering things sometimes? For example, do you have trouble remembering where you put your keys or if you turned off the stove?

Make a list of things you have trouble remembering. Then share your list with the class.

I sometimes have trouble remembering . . .

- _____
- _____
- _____

B. You are going to hear a story about a woman who had a problem with her memory. Look at the picture. Where did she go for help?

🎧 Look at the pictures as you listen to the story.

❸ CHECKING YOUR UNDERSTANDING

🎧 A. Listen to the story again. As you listen, read the story below. There are five mistakes in the story. Cross out the mistakes. (The first one is done for you.)

A woman had a memory problem, so she went to a ~~teacher~~.

"Doctor," the woman said. "I have a back problem. I park my motorcycle somewhere, and I can't find it. I put my glasses somewhere, and I can't find them. I put my cat somewhere, and I can't find him."

"Hmmm," the doctor said. "This *is* serious. Write me more about your problem."

"Problem?" the woman said. "What problem?"

B. Write the missing word on the line. Check your answers in the Answer Key. Then sit with a partner and read the conversation aloud. Student A begins.

A	B
1. So . . . you have a problem?	Yes, I have a problem with my _____*memory*_____.
2. Can you give me an example?	Well, sometimes I _____ my car somewhere, and I can't find it.
3. You can't find your car?	No, I can't find it. And I put my _____ somewhere, and I can't find them.
4. You can't _____ your glasses?	No, I can't find them. And I put my baby _____, and I can't find him.
5. You can't find your baby?	No, I can't find _____.
6. This *is* serious. Tell me more _____ your problem.	Problem? What problem?

❹ LISTENING AND WRITING

⌒ Cover the sentences below with a piece of paper. You will hear the sentences. As you listen, write them on the lines. Then lift your paper and check your writing.

1. A woman had a memory problem.

2. She told the doctor about her problem.

3. The woman couldn't find her car, her glasses, or her baby.

4. The doctor wanted to know more.

5. The woman didn't remember her problem.

1. _____

2. _____

3. _____

4. _____

5. _____

❺ RETELLING THE STORY

A. Write the story in your own words on the lines. Use the keywords to help you.

• woman, go, doctor

• have, memory problem

• park, car, somewhere, can't find

• put, glasses, somewhere, can't find

• put, baby, somewhere, can't find

• tell, more

• what problem

_____

_____

_____

_____

_____

_____

_____

_____

_____

_____

_____

_____

_____

_____

B. Tell the story to a partner. Use the pictures on the LISTENING TO THE STORY page to help you.

❻ TALKING ABOUT THE TOPIC

How Can You Improve Your Memory?

A. Try this experiment:

1. Look at the list below for one minute. Then close your book. How many words can you remember? Write the words. (Most people remember between four and eight words. Younger people usually remember more words than older people.)

balloon	river
doctor	potato
hat	horse
newspaper	lamp
soap	ear

2. Read the story below two or three times. Try to remember the story.

A *doctor* turned on a *lamp*. Then he sat down to read a *newspaper*. After he read the newspaper, he saw that his hands were dirty. So he went into the bathroom and washed his hands with *soap*. While he was in the bathroom, he looked out the window and saw a beautiful *balloon*. He wanted the balloon, so he put on his *hat* and went outside. When he went outside, he saw a *horse*. He got on the horse and said into the horse's *ear*, "Follow that balloon." He rode the horse across a *river*. But the doctor never found the balloon. So he went home and ate a *potato* for dinner.

3. Close your book. Think about the story. Now try to remember the words on the list and write them. Were you able to remember more words?

4. Repeat the experiment with the list below. Look at the list for one minute and try to remember the words. How many words did you remember? In a small group, write a story using all the words. (Don't worry if your story doesn't make sense.) Think about the story. Then try to remember the words on the list. Can you remember more words?

baby

key

taxi

cake

rain

spoon

pants

dog

clock

ball

B. It is easier for most people to remember words if the words are in a story. Do you have other ways of remembering things? Share your ideas with the class. (There are more ideas for remembering things in the Answer Key.)

UNIT 4
The Test

❶ BEFORE LISTENING

A. Read the following sentences.

> She can play basketball, and he can play basketball too.
> She can't swim, and he can't swim either.
>
> I speak Chinese, and they speak Chinese too.
> I don't speak French, and they don't speak French either.

When do you use *too*, and when do you use *either*? Talk it over with the class. Then check your understanding of the two words. Complete the sentences below with *too* or *either*. Write your answer on the line. Then check your answers in the Answer Key.

1. We have a lot of homework, and they have a lot of homework _____*too*_____.

2. She can't come to the party, and he can't come to the party _____.

3. This TV isn't expensive, and that one isn't expensive _____.

4. I like vanilla ice cream, and he likes it _____.

5. She doesn't know the answer, and he doesn't know the answer _____.

B. You are going to hear a story about a boy who got a zero on a test. Look at the picture. Why do you think the boy's teacher gave him a zero?

❷ LISTENING TO THE STORY

🎧 Look at the pictures as you listen to the story.

❸ CHECKING YOUR UNDERSTANDING

🎧 **A. Listen to the story again. As you listen, write the missing word on the line.**

A student got a zero on a _____ *test* _____. "Why did you give me a

_____ ₂ _____?" he asked the teacher. "Most of my _____ ₃ _____ are correct."

"Yes, but you _____ ₄ _____ Mary's answers," the teacher said.

"That's true," the student said. "How _____ ₅ _____ you know?"

"Well," said the teacher, "your answers and Mary's answers are the _____ ₆ _____.

Only answer number seven is _____ ₇ _____. Mary wrote, 'I don't know,' and you

_____ ₈ _____ 'I don't know either.'"

B. Write the missing word on the line. Check your answers in the Answer Key. Then sit with a partner and read the conversation aloud. Student A begins.

A	B
1. I have a question about my grade.	Yes?
2. You _____ *gave* _____ me a zero on the test.	That's right.
3. Why did you give me a zero? _____ of my answers are correct.	Yes, but you copied Mary's _____.
4. That's true. How did you _____?	Your answers and her answers are the same. Only answer number seven is different. Mary _____, "I don't know," and you wrote, "I don't know either."

❹ LISTENING AND WRITING

🎧 **Cover the sentences below with a piece of paper. You will hear the sentences. As you listen, write them on the lines. Then lift your paper and check your writing.**

1. The student copied Mary's answers.

2. Their answers were the same.

3. Only number seven was different.

4. Mary wrote that she didn't know.

5. The student wrote that he didn't know either.

6. The teacher gave the student a zero on the test.

1. _____

2. _____

3. _____

4. _____

5. _____

6. _____

❺ RETELLING THE STORY

A. Write the story in your own words on the lines. Use the keywords to help you.

• student, get, zero

• ask, teacher, why, give, zero

• most, answers, correct

• copy, Mary's answers

• how, know

• answers, same

- only number seven, different
- Mary, write, don't know
- you, write, don't know, either

_____

_____

_____

_____

_____

_____

_____

_____

_____

_____

_____

_____

_____

B. Tell the story to a partner. Use the pictures on the LISTENING TO THE STORY page to help you.

❻ TALKING ABOUT THE TOPIC

How Do Students Cheat?

A student tried to cheat using the water bottle in the photo. The answers to a test are on the back of the label. The teacher saw the answers and took the bottle. The student got a zero on the test.

A. Make a list of ways students cheat. For example:

• *They copy someone's answers.*
• *They write answers on the bottoms of their shoes.*

Write your list here. Then share your list with the class.

• _____

• _____

• _____

B. In your country, what happens to students who cheat? Tell the class.

You've Changed

❶ BEFORE LISTENING

A. Read about a woman named Misuk.

Misuk used to live in South Korea, but now she lives in the United States. Her life in the United States is very different from her life in South Korea. She used to live in a big city. Now she lives in a small town. She used to take the subway to work. Now she drives a car. She used to live with her parents. Now she lives with two roommates.

Think about the expression "used to." When do you use it? Talk it over with the class. Then complete the sentence below. Write your answer on the line. Share your sentence with the class.

I used to _____, but now I _____.

(For example: I used to __*get up late*__, but now I __*get up early*__.)

B. You are going to hear a story about the man in the picture. Read the sentences below. If the sentence describes the man, circle *T* for *true*. If the sentence does not describe the man, circle *F* for *false*.

1. He is thin.   (T)   F
2. He wears glasses.   T   F
3. He has black hair.   T   F
4. He is heavy.   T   F
5. He has gray hair.   T   F

🎧 Look at the pictures as you listen to the story.

❸ CHECKING YOUR UNDERSTANDING

🎧 **A. Listen to the story again. As you listen, write the missing word on the line.**

Mr. Mix was walking down the _____ *street* _____ when he met another man. "Mr.
1
Peterson!" said Mr. Mix. "You've _____! You look very different. You used to
2
be heavy, and _____ you're thin. You used to _____ black hair,
3   4
and now you have gray hair. You _____ to wear glasses, and now you
5
don't."

"I'm not Mr. Peterson," said the man. "_____ Mr. Jones."
6

"Wow!" said Mr. Mix. "You've changed your name _____!"
7

**B. Write the missing word on the line. Check your answers in the Answer Key. Then sit
with a partner and read the conversation aloud. Student A begins.**

A	B

1. Hello!

2. I haven't seen you for a long time.

3. Sure you do! I'm Mr. _____ *Mix* _____.

4. You've changed! The last time I saw
   you, you were _____.

5. And you had black hair.

6. And you _____ glasses.

7. Well, I have to go. It was nice seeing
   you again, Mr. Peterson.

8. Wow! You've changed your
   _____ too!

Hello.

I'm sorry. I don't think I know you.

I'm sorry, Mr. Mix. I don't remember you.

Really? Well, I've lost a few pounds.

Black _____? That
was a long time ago.

Glasses? That's strange. I've
never worn glasses.

Mr. Peterson? I'm _____
Mr. Peterson. I'm Mr. Jones.

❹ LISTENING AND WRITING

🎧 **Cover the sentences below with a piece of paper. You will hear the sentences.
As you listen, write them on the lines. Then lift your paper and check your writing.**

1. Mr. Mix met a man on the street.

2. He thought the man was Mr. Peterson.

3. He said the man had changed.

4. He used to be heavy, but now he is thin.

5. He used to have black hair, but now he has gray hair.

6. He used to wear glasses, but now he doesn't.

7. The man said he was Mr. Jones, not Mr. Peterson.

8. Mr. Mix thought the man had changed his name too.

1. _____

2. _____

3. _____

4. _____

5. _____

6. _____

7. _____

8. _____

❺ RETELLING THE STORY

A. Write the story in your own words on the lines. Use the keywords to help you.

- Mr. Mix, walk, street, meet, man

- Mr. Peterson, change

- used to be, heavy, now, thin

- used to have, black hair, now, gray

- used to wear, glasses, now, don't

- man, say, not Mr. Peterson, Mr. Jones

- change, name, too

_____

_____

_____

_____

_____

_____

_____

_____

_____

_____

_____

_____

_____

_____

_____

_____

**B. Tell the story to a partner. Use the pictures on the LISTENING TO THE STORY
page to help you.**

❻ TALKING ABOUT THE TOPIC

Have You Changed?

Draw a picture of yourself looking the way you used to look or doing something you used to do. Then write a few sentences about your picture. For example:

- I used to wear long pants like these.
- One pant leg was one color, and the other pant leg was another color.
- I used to wear a baseball hat every day.
- I used to have long hair.

Now draw your picture on your own paper. Write a few sentences about your picture on the lines. Then show your picture to the class. Describe to the class how you have changed.

_____

_____

_____

_____

_____

_____

_____

_____

The New Job

❶ BEFORE LISTENING

A. Imagine this: Two people are talking. You can't hear all the words of their conversation, but you can hear some words. These are the words you hear:

> hours . . .   coffee break . . .   lunch break . . .   pay . . .   vacation . . .
> health insurance . . .   start . . .

What do you think the people are talking about? Tell the class.

B. You are going to hear a story about a man who has found a new job. Look at the picture. How do you think his wife feels about the new job?

❷ LISTENING TO THE STORY

🎧 Look at the pictures as you listen to the story.

❸ CHECKING YOUR UNDERSTANDING

🎧 **A. Listen to the story again. As you listen, complete the sentences. Circle the letter of your answer.**

1. The hours are from
   a. eight in the morning to five o'clock in the afternoon.
   b. seven in the morning to four o'clock in the afternoon.

2. There are
   a. three coffee breaks.
   b. two coffee breaks.

3. The lunch break is
   a. a half hour.
   b. one hour.

4. The pay is
   a. good.
   b. excellent.

5. The health insurance is
   a. free.
   b. fifty dollars a month.

6. The vacation is
   a. two weeks.
   b. three weeks.

B. Write the missing word on the line. Check your answers in the Answer Key. Then sit with a partner and read the conversation aloud. Student A begins.

A	B
1. Guess what! I've found a great ___job___!	Good! Tell me about it.
2. The _____ are from eight to five.	That's good. Is there a lunch break?
3. Yes, it's an hour.	That's good. Are _____ coffee breaks?
4. Yes, there are two—one in the morning and one in the _____.	That's good. Is there health _____?

5. Yes, there's health insurance, and it's

   _____.

   That's good. Is there a vacation?

6. Yes, there's a three-week vacation.

   The job sounds great! I'm very,

   very _____!

7. Good! You start _____.

④ LISTENING AND WRITING

🎧 **Cover the sentences below with a piece of paper. You will hear the sentences.
As you listen, write them on the lines. Then lift your paper and check your writing.**

1. A man told his wife about a great job.

2. The hours are from eight to five.

3. There are two coffee breaks.

4. The lunch break is one hour.

5. The pay is excellent.

6. There is free health insurance.

7. There is a three-week vacation.

8. He told his wife she starts tomorrow.

1. _____

2. _____

3. _____

4. _____

5. _____

6. _____

7. _____

8. _____

❺ RETELLING THE STORY

A. Write the story in your own words on the lines. Use the keywords to help you.

- come home, run into the house
- tell, wife, find, job
- hours, eight o'clock in the morning, five o'clock in the afternoon
- two coffee breaks
- one-hour lunch break
- pay, excellent
- free health insurance
- three-week vacation
- think
- sound great, happy
- good, start tomorrow

_____

_____

_____

_____

_____

_____

_____

_____

_____

_____

_____

_____

_____

_____

_____

B. Tell the story to a partner. Use the pictures on the LISTENING TO THE STORY page to help you.

⑥ TALKING ABOUT THE TOPIC

What Is a Great Job?

Complete the sentences. Write your answer on the line. Then share your answers with the class.

1. Where is the work? (for example: in an office, in a factory, in a restaurant, outdoors)

   The work is _____.

2. What are the hours? (for example: from nine o'clock to five o'clock)

   The hours are _____.

3. How long is the lunch break? (for example: one hour)

   The lunch break is _____.

4. How many coffee breaks are there? (for example: two)

   There are _____.

5. What is the pay? (for example: eighteen dollars an hour)

   The pay is _____.

6. How long is the vacation? (for example: two weeks)

   The vacation is _____.

At the Barbershop

❶ BEFORE LISTENING

A. Look at the photo of the man at the barbershop. What do men get at a barbershop? Tell the class.

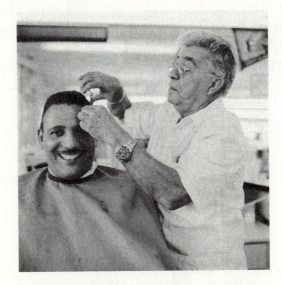

B. You are going to hear a story about a man who got a manicure at a barbershop. Look at the picture. What was the man thinking about?

❷ LISTENING TO THE STORY

🎧 Look at the pictures as you listen to the story.

❸ CHECKING YOUR UNDERSTANDING

🎧 **A. Listen to the story again. As you listen, circle the correct word.**

1. Dan was at a ((barbershop) / library).

2. He was getting a manicure and a (haircut / shave).

3. A young (man / woman) was giving him a manicure.

4. Dan decided to ask her for (a date / her phone number).

5. "Are you free for (lunch / dinner) tonight?" he asked her.

6. "I (can't / can) have dinner with you," the woman answered.

7. "I have a (husband / boyfriend)."

8. Dan said, "Tell your boyfriend you're having dinner with (your mother /

   a girlfriend)."

9. "You tell him," the woman said. "He's (helping / shaving) you."

B. Write the missing word on the line. Check your answers in the Answer Key. Then sit with a partner and read the conversation aloud. Student A begins.

A	B
1. Are you free for dinner __tonight__?	I'm sorry. I can't have dinner with you. I _____ a boyfriend.
2. That's not a problem.	It isn't?
3. No, it isn't.	Why not?
4. You can call your boyfriend. Tell him you're having _____ with a girlfriend.	You _____ him. He's shaving you.

④ LISTENING AND WRITING

🎧 Cover the sentences below with a piece of paper. You will hear the sentences. As you listen, write them on the lines. Then lift your paper and check your writing.

1. Dan was at a barbershop.

2. He was getting a manicure and a shave.

3. A young woman was giving him a manicure.

4. Dan asked her for a date.

5. She couldn't have dinner with Dan.

6. She had a boyfriend.

7. The boyfriend was shaving Dan.

1. _____

2. _____

3. _____

4. _____

5. _____

6. _____

7. _____

⑤ RETELLING THE STORY

A. Write the story in your own words on the lines. Use the keywords to help you.

• barbershop

• get, manicure, shave

• young woman, give, manicure

• young man, shave

• like, woman

• ask for, date

• free, dinner

- sorry, can't
- have, boyfriend
- can
- call, boyfriend
- tell, dinner, girlfriend
- you, tell
- shave you

_____

_____

_____

_____

_____

_____

_____

_____

_____

_____

_____

_____

_____

_____

B. Tell the story to a partner. Use the pictures on the LISTENING TO THE STORY
page to help you.

6 TALKING ABOUT THE TOPIC

How Do You Invite Someone to Do Something?

Practice inviting someone to do something. Also practice saying "yes" and "no" to an invitation. Follow these steps:

1. Think about what words can you use to invite someone to do something. Make a list. Your teacher will write your list on the board. For example:

   Are you free . . .

   Would you like to . . .

2. Think about what you can invite someone to do. Make a second list. Your teacher will write your list on the board. For example:

   play tennis

   go to a movie

3. Think about what reasons people give when they say "no" to an invitation. Make a third list. Your teacher will write your list on the board. For example:

   I have to work.

   I already have plans.

4. Think about what people say when they say "yes" to an invitation. Make a fourth list. For example:

   I'd love to.

   That sounds great.

5. Now sit with a partner. Practice inviting someone to do something, and practice saying "yes" and "no." Use the phrases on the board.

UNIT 8

Two Ships in the Night

❶ BEFORE LISTENING

A. Look at the photo. Which words do you think might be in the next story? Circle five words. (The first one is done for you.)

(ship)
bicycle
water
teacher
captain
road
pencil
boat
radio

B. You are going to hear a story about a captain who saw a light ahead of his ship. Look at the picture. What did he think the light was?

❷ LISTENING TO THE STORY

🎧 Look at the pictures as you listen to the story.

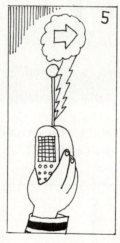

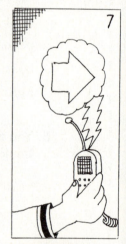

❸ CHECKING YOUR UNDERSTANDING

🎧 **A. Listen to the story again. As you listen, write the missing word on the line.**

Late at night, a big ship was going through the _____*water*_____. The captain saw a
1

_____ ahead. "It's a boat," he thought.
2

He picked _____ the radio. "Move to your right," he said.
3

The answer came back: "No, *you* move to *your* _____."
4

The captain picked up the radio _____. "Move to your right!" he said.
5

The _____ came back: "No, *you* move to *your* right!"
6

The captain picked up the radio again. "Move to your right!" he _____.
7

"This is a big ship!"

The answer came back: "Yes, you are a big _____. And this is a big
8

lighthouse."

**B. Write the missing word on the line. Check your answers in the Answer Key. Then sit
with a partner and read the conversation aloud. Student A begins.**

A	B

1. This is the captain speaking.   Yes, I can _____*hear*_____ you.

   Can you hear me?

2. I see you ahead of me.   Yes, I see you too.

3. You need to move to your   No, *you* need to move to *your*

   _____.   right.

4. Move to your right!   No, *you* _____

         to *your* right!

5. You don't understand: This is a   *You* don't understand: This is a

   _____ ship!   big _____!

❹ LISTENING AND WRITING

🎧 Cover the sentences below with a piece of paper. You will hear the sentences. As you listen, write them on the lines. Then lift your paper and check your writing.

1. The captain of a ship saw a light.

2. He thought it was a boat.

3. He picked up his radio and told the boat to move.

4. He got an answer back.

5. A man told him to move.

6. The captain was angry.

7. He said that his ship was big.

8. The man said the lighthouse was big too.

1. _____

2. _____

3. _____

4. _____

5. _____

6. _____

7. _____

8. _____

❺ RETELLING THE STORY

A. Write the story in your own words on the lines. Use the keywords to help you.

• night, ship, water

• captain, see, light

• pick up, radio

• move, right

• answer, you, move

- pick up, radio, again
- move, right
- answer, you, move
- pick up, radio, again
- move, right, shout
- big ship
- big lighthouse

_____

_____

_____

_____

_____

_____

_____

_____

_____

_____

_____

_____

_____

B. Tell the story to a partner. Use the pictures on the LISTENING TO THE STORY page to help you.

⑥ TALKING ABOUT THE TOPIC

Can You Always Believe What You See?

The captain thought he saw a boat, but it was a lighthouse. Things are not always what they seem!

Look at the pictures below.[1] Answer the questions. Tell the class your answers.

1. Is it a bird or a rabbit?

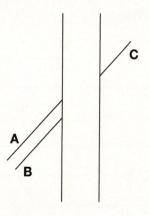

2. Which line connects to C—A or B?

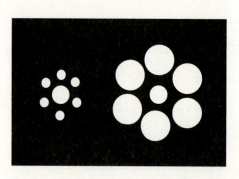

3. Which center circle is bigger— the one on the left or the one on the right?

4. Do you see a vase for flowers, or do you see two faces?

---

[1]Pictures like these are called *optical illusions.* There are many examples on the Internet. To find them, go to a search engine and type in "optical illusions."

UNIT 9
The Loan

❶ BEFORE LISTENING

A. Complete the sentences. Write your answer on the line.

> wallets   loan   bandits   rob   jewelry   passengers

1. The men in the picture below are _____bandits_____.

2. The men in the picture take people's money. They _____ people.

3. The people riding on a bus, a train, or an airplane are the _____.

4. Rings, earrings, and necklaces are _____.

5. People keep their money in their _____.

6. Your friend's pencil breaks during a test, so you give your friend a pencil. After

   the test, your friend will give the pencil back to you. You _____ your

   friend a pencil.

B. You are going to hear a story about two friends who were riding on a bus. Look at the picture. Who got on the bus?

❷ LISTENING TO THE STORY

🎧 Look at the pictures as you listen to the story.

❸ CHECKING YOUR UNDERSTANDING

🎧 **A. Listen to the story again. As you listen, write the missing word on the line.**

Two friends, Sam and Mike, were _____*riding*_____ on a bus. Suddenly, the bus
                                              1

stopped and bandits _____ on. The bandits began robbing the
                          2

passengers. They were taking the passengers' jewelry and _____. They
                                                                    3

were taking all their money too.

Sam opened his _____ and took out twenty dollars. He gave the
                      4

twenty dollars to Mike.

"Why are you giving me this _____?" Mike asked.
                                    5

"Last week I didn't have _____ money, and you loaned me twenty
                                6

dollars, remember?" Sam said.

"Yes, I _____," Mike said.
              7

"I'm paying you _____," Sam said.
                      8

**B. Complete the sentences. Write your answer on the line. Check your answers in the
Answer Key. Then sit with a partner. Student A asks the question; student B
answers.**

1. **A.** Two friends were riding on a train, right?

   B. No, they were riding on a _____*bus*_____.

2. **A.** Suddenly the bus stopped and the police got on, right?

   B. No, suddenly the bus stopped and _____.

3. **A.** The bandits began helping the passengers, right?

   B. No, they began _____.

4. **A.** They began taking the passengers' jackets, sweaters, and shoes, right?

   B. No, they began taking their _____.

5. **A.** Sam opened his wallet and took out ten dollars, right?

   B. No, he opened his wallet and took out _____.

6. **A.** He gave the twenty dollars to the bandits, right?

   B. No, he gave the twenty dollars to _____.

7. **A.** He told Mike, "Last year you loaned me twenty dollars," right?

    B. No, he told him, "Last _____."

8. **A.** He said, "I'm calling you back," right?

    B. No, he said, "I'm _____."

❹ LISTENING AND WRITING

🎧 **Cover the sentences below with a piece of paper. You will hear the sentences. As you listen, write them on the lines. Then lift your paper and check your writing.**

1. Sam and Mike were riding on a bus.

2. Bandits were robbing the passengers.

3. Sam opened his wallet.

4. He took out twenty dollars.

5. He gave the money to Mike.

6. Why was Sam giving Mike money?

7. Mike had loaned him twenty dollars.

8. He was paying Mike back.

1. _____

2. _____

3. _____

4. _____

5. _____

6. _____

7. _____

8. _____

⑤ RETELLING THE STORY

A. Write the story in your own words on the lines. Use the keywords to help you.

- Sam, Mike, ride, bus
- bus, stop, bandits, get on
- bandits, rob, passengers
- take, jewelry, watches, money
- Sam, open, wallet, take out, twenty dollars

- give, money, Mike
- Mike, ask, why, give, money
- Sam, say, last week, loan, twenty dollars
- pay back

_____

_____

_____

_____

_____

_____

_____

_____

_____

_____

_____

_____

_____

_____

_____

_____

_____

B. Tell the story to a partner. Use the pictures on the LISTENING TO THE STORY page to help you.

❻ TALKING ABOUT THE TOPIC

Is It a Good Idea to Loan Things?

A. What things have you loaned people? Check (✓) your answers. Share your answers with the class. Who do you often loan things to? A friend? A relative? A neighbor? Tell the class.

❑ an umbrella

❑ a book

❑ a pot for cooking

❑ food (some eggs to a neighbor, for example)

❑ laundry detergent

❑ a bicycle

❑ some furniture (a chair, for example)

❑ a car

❑ a camera

❑ a comb

❑ jewelry

❑ a hair dryer

❑ a video game

❑ a music CD

❑ a movie on tape or on DVD

❑ clothes

❑ a suitcase

❑ a tool

❑ an identification card

❑ money

❑ _____

(other)

B. Write about an experience you've had with loaning something to someone. For example:

My cousin said she wanted to learn English. I loaned her my English book. She never used the book and she didn't learn English. She didn't give the book back to me.

Now write about your experience in the space below. Then tell the class about it.

_____

_____

_____

_____

_____

_____

The Long and Happy Marriage

❶ BEFORE LISTENING

A. Complete the sentences with the words below. Write your answer on the line.

reporter   twice   couple   marriage   secret   wedding anniversary

1. Two people who are in love (for example: boyfriend and girlfriend, husband and wife) are a _____*couple*_____.

2. If you get married on May 12, then every year May 12 is your

    _____.

3. A person who writes for a newspaper is a _____.

4. Your friend makes delicious spaghetti. You think your friend knows the best way to make it. So you ask your friend, "What is your _____ for making delicious spaghetti?"

5. If you have been married for a long time and you are happy, then you have a long and happy _____.

6. Another way to say "two times every day" is "_____ a day."

B. You are going to hear a story about a reporter who wants to write a story about an old couple. Look at the picture. What do you think the reporter wants to know?

🎧 Look at the pictures as you listen to the story.

❸ CHECKING YOUR UNDERSTANDING

🎧 **A. Listen to the story again. As you listen, circle the correct words.**

1. It was a special day for ((an old)/ a young couple.)

2. It was their (fiftieth / fortieth) wedding anniversary.

3. They were very (happy / unhappy) together.

4. A (newspaper / TV) reporter went to their house.

5. "Tell me," the reporter said. "What is the secret of your long and happy

   (marriage / lives)?"

6. The old (man / woman) answered.

7. "Twice a (week / month), we go to a romantic restaurant," he said.

8. "We (drive / take a long walk) to the restaurant."

9. "After dinner, we drink (coffee / tea) and listen to the music."

10. "She goes on Tuesdays, and I go on (Saturdays / Fridays)."

B. Answer the questions. Write your answer on the line. Check your answers in the Answer Key. Then sit with a partner. Student A asks the question; student B answers.

1. **A.** Why was it a special day for the old couple?

   B. _It was their fiftieth wedding anniversary._

2. **A.** Who went to their house?

   B. _____

3. **A.** Why did the reporter go there?

   B. _____

4. **A.** What did the reporter ask?

   B. _____

5. **A.** Where does the couple go?

   B. _____

6. **A.** How often do they go?

   B. _____

7. **A.** What do they do after dinner?

   B. _____

8. **A.** When does the man go, and when does the woman go?

   B. _____

✅ LISTENING AND WRITING

🎧 **Cover the sentences below with a piece of paper. You will hear the sentences. As you listen, write them on the lines. Then lift your paper and check your writing.**

1. An old couple was very happy.

2. It was their fiftieth wedding anniversary.

3. A reporter wanted to know their secret.

4. The old man said they go to a romantic restaurant twice a week.

5. They take a long walk to the restaurant.

6. They eat a delicious dinner and listen to music.

7. He goes on Fridays.

8. His wife goes on Tuesdays.

1. _____

2. _____

3. _____

4. _____

5. _____

6. _____

7. _____

8. _____

⑤ RETELLING THE STORY

A. Write the story in your own words on the lines. Use the keywords to help you.

- special day, old couple
- fiftieth wedding anniversary
- happy
- newspaper reporter, go, house
- want, write, story
- tell, secret, long and happy marriage

- twice a week, romantic restaurant
- long walk
- delicious dinner
- drink, coffee, listen to, music
- long walk, home
- Tuesdays, Fridays

_____

_____

_____

_____

_____

_____

_____

_____

_____

_____

_____

_____

_____

_____

_____

_____

B. Tell the story to a partner. Use the pictures on the LISTENING TO THE STORY page to help you.

❻ TALKING ABOUT THE TOPIC

What Is Your Secret for a Long and Happy Marriage?

That is the question BBC News asked. People e-mailed their ideas, and the BBC put their ideas on the Internet.

A. Read the ideas. Then give your opinion of each idea. Give each idea one, two, or three stars.

> *** = *excellent idea; very important*
> ** = *good idea; important*
> * = *not a good idea; not important*

1. _____ Never go to bed angry.   (Caroline, UK)

2. _____ Tell your husband/wife that you love them, first thing in the morning and last thing at night.   (Wendy, UK)

3. _____ Don't argue about small things. Every time you argue, ask, "Will this really matter two years from now?"   (Peter, USA)

4. _____ Laugh a lot.   (David, USA)

5. _____ Don't try to change your husband/wife.   (Steve, UK)

6. _____ Don't spend too much time together. Spend some time alone or with other people.   (Jim, USA)

7. _____ Move far away from your mother-in-law. (Claire, UK)

8. _____ Be honest; never lie.   (Michael, UK)

9. _____ Have a special time together every week. Take a walk or drink a cup of tea together, for example. During that time, do not talk about family problems, and do not talk about money.   (Teri, USA)

10. _____

(Write your own idea.)

Now share your answers with a partner. Do you and your partner have the same opinions?

B. Of all the ideas above, which do you think is the most important? Why do you think it is important? Complete the sentence below. Then share your answer with the class.

I think idea # _____ is the most important because _____

_____.

The Mean Boss

❶ BEFORE LISTENING

A. Complete the sentences. Write the letter of your answer on the line.

1. Your neighbor is not nice.

   Your neighbor is ___e___

2. Your friend works ten hours a day.

   Your friend works _____

3. You want people to leave a building fast.

   You tell them to _____

4. Your mail is at the post office, so you go there and get it.

   You _____

5. You like your work.

   You have a good _____

a. hard.

b. get out.

c. job.

d. pick it up.

e. mean.

B. You are going to hear a story about a boss who liked to watch his workers. Look at the picture. The boss was angry. Why?

❷ LISTENING TO THE STORY

🎧 Look at the pictures as you listen to the story.

❸ CHECKING YOUR UNDERSTANDING

🎧 **A. Listen to the story again. As you listen, write the missing word on the line.**

There was a mean _____*boss*_____ in a factory. The boss liked to

_____ the workers. He wanted the workers to work hard.

2

One morning the boss came to the factory at nine _____. A man was

3
drinking coffee. The boss came back at 9:30. The man was _____ drinking

4
coffee. The boss was angry. "How much do you _____ a week?" he asked

5
the man.

"Seven hundred dollars," the man said.

The boss _____ the man seven hundred dollars. "Take the money and

6
get _____ of here," he said.

7

Then the boss asked another worker, "What was that man's _____?"

8

"He _____ work here," the worker said. "He came to pick up a

9
_____."

10

B. Answer the questions. Write your answer on the line. Check your answers in the Answer Key. Then sit with a partner. Student A reads the question; student B answers.

1. **A.** The boss was nice, right?

   B. No, he was _____*mean*_____.

2. **A.** He liked to watch the workers in his office, right?

   B. No, he liked to watch the workers in his _____.

3. **A.** He saw a man drinking water, right?

   B. No, he saw a man drinking _____.

4. **A.** The boss was happy, right?

   B. No, he was _____.

5. **A.** He asked the man, "How much do you make a month," right?

   B. No, he asked him, "How much do you make a _____?"

6. **A.** The man said, "Four hundred dollars," right?

   B. No, he said, "_____."

7. **A.** The boss said, "Take the money and buy more coffee," right?

   B. No, he said, "Take the money and _____."

8. **A.** The man came to fix a machine, right?

   B. No, he came to _____.

❹ LISTENING AND WRITING

🎧 **Cover the sentences below with a piece of paper. You will hear the sentences. As you listen, write them on the lines. Then lift your paper and check your writing.**

1. A mean boss liked to watch the workers.

2. One morning he saw a man drinking coffee.

3. The man drank coffee for thirty minutes.

4. The boss gave the man seven hundred dollars.

5. He told the man to leave.

6. The man didn't work at the factory.

7. He was at the factory to pick up a package.

1. _____

2. _____

3. _____

4. _____

5. _____

6. _____

7. _____

❺ RETELLING THE STORY

A. Write the story in your own words on the lines. Use the keywords to help you.

- mean boss, factory
- like, watch, workers
- want, workers, work, hard
- one morning, come, factory, nine o'clock
- drink, coffee
- come back, 9:30
- still drink, coffee

- ask, how much, a week
- seven hundred dollars
- give
- take money, get out
- ask, worker, man's job
- work here, pick up, package

_____

_____

_____

_____

_____

_____

_____

_____

_____

_____

_____

_____

_____

_____

B. Tell the story to a partner. Use the pictures on the LISTENING TO THE STORY page to help you.

⑥ TALKING ABOUT THE TOPIC

What Is the Ideal Boss?

The boss in the story was a "mean boss," the opposite of an ideal boss.

Think about the place where you are working now. Also think about places where you have worked in the past. Now think about your bosses. Which bosses did you like? Why did you like them?

Complete the sentences. For example:

- The ideal boss _____ *shows employees how to do the work.* _____
- The ideal boss _____ *gives extra money to employees who work hard.* _____

Now complete the sentences.

- The ideal boss _____.
- The ideal boss _____.
- The ideal boss _____.

Share your sentences with the class. If you have a story about a good boss or a bad boss, tell the class.

Dear John

❶ BEFORE LISTENING

A. Match the sentences. Write the letter of your answer on the line.

1. There are three books for this class. __b__   **a.** Which one doesn't have meat?

2. There are four men in the photo. _____   **b.** Which one will we read first?

3. There are six pizzas on the table. _____   **c.** Which one is your brother?

4. There are three movies at the theater. _____   **d.** Which one do you want to see?

Think about the expression "which one." When do you use it? Talk it over with the class.

B. You are going to read a story about a soldier who got a letter. Look at the picture. Who do you think the letter was from?

⌐ Look at the pictures as you listen to the story.

❸ CHECKING YOUR UNDERSTANDING

🎧 **A. Listen to the story again. As you listen, read the story below. There are six mistakes in the story. Cross out the mistakes. (The first one is done for you.)**

A young soldier was far away from home. One day he got a letter from his ~~mother~~.

The letter said:

> Dear Michael,
>
>   I am sorry, but I have new boyfriend. You have a very nice picture of me. Please send it back. I want to give it to my new boyfriend.
>
>   Maria

The soldier was happy. He asked his friends for pictures of men—aunts, sisters, girlfriends, mothers, or cousins. He put the pictures of the women in a big box, and he sent the box to his girlfriend. In the box he also put a present. The letter said:

> Dear Maria,
>
>   Please take your ring. I can't remember which one you are.
>
>   John

B. Answer the questions. Write your answer on the line. Check your answers in the Answer Key. Then sit with a partner. Student A asks the question; student B answers.

1. **A.** Where was the soldier?

   B. _He was far away from home._

2. **A.** What did he get one day?

   B. _____

3. **A.** Why did Maria want her picture back?

   B. _____

4. **A.** How did the soldier feel?

   B. _____

5. **A.** What did the soldier's friends give him?

   B. _____

6. **A.** Where did he put the pictures?

   B. _____

7. **A.** What else did he put in the box?

   B. _____

8. **A.** What did the letter say?

   B. _____

❹ LISTENING AND WRITING

🎧 **Cover the sentences below with a piece of paper. You will hear the sentences. As you listen, write them on the lines. Then lift your paper and check your writing.**

1. A soldier got a letter from his girlfriend.

2. She wanted her picture back.

3. She wanted to give it to her new boyfriend.

4. The soldier was angry.

5. He asked his friends for pictures of women.

6. He sent the pictures to his girlfriend.

7. He told her to take her picture.

8. He said he couldn't remember who she was.

1. _____

2. _____

3. _____

4. _____

5. _____

6. _____

7. _____

8. _____

⑤ RETELLING THE STORY

A. Write the story in your own words on the lines. Use the keywords to help you.

- soldier, far away

- get letter, girlfriend

- sorry, boyfriend

- have, nice picture, send back

- give, new boyfriend

- angry

- ask, friends, pictures, women

- put, box

- send, box, girlfriend

- put, letter

- take, picture

- can't remember, which one

_____

_____

_____

_____

_____

_____

_____

_____

_____

_____

_____

_____

_____

_____

B. Tell the story to a partner. Use the pictures on the LISTENING TO THE STORY page to help you.

❻ TALKING ABOUT THE TOPIC

How Do You End a Romance?

A. Maria broke up with John because she had a new boyfriend. What are some reasons people break up? Tell the class.

B. Compare your experiences with breaking up with other people's experiences.

The questions below were on an Internet Web site. First, answer the questions. Circle the letter of your answer. Next, share your answers with the class. Finally, read the answers people in the United States gave on the Web site. (Their answers are in the Answer Key.)

1. What is the best way to break up with someone?
   a. in person
   b. on the phone
   c. in a letter
   d. in e-mail
   e. through a friend
   f. _____

   (other)

2. Who, in your experience, usually ends a romance—the man or the woman?
   a. the man
   b. the woman
   c. sometimes the man, sometimes the woman

3. Which is more difficult—when you break up with someone, or when someone breaks up with you?
   a. when I break up with someone
   b. when someone breaks up with me

4. What is the reason most people give when they break up with someone?
   a. "I'm not in love with you."
   b. "I'm in love with someone else."
   c. "I'm not ready to have a serious romance now."
   d. "We don't have the same religion."
   e. "My family doesn't want us to be together."
   f. "We fight too much."
   g. _____

   (other)

UNIT 13
The Parking Space

❶ BEFORE LISTENING

A. Look at the photos. Two cars like these are in the next story.

Which words do you think might be in the story? Circle eight words. (The first one is done for you.)

(drive)	crash	back up
parking lot	sports car	airplane
write	cook	insurance
book	reverse	
parking space	jump	

B. You are going to hear a story about a woman who is looking for something. Look at the picture. What is she looking for?

🎧 Look at the pictures as you listen to the story.

❸ CHECKING YOUR UNDERSTANDING

🎧 A. Listen to the story again. As you listen, write the missing word on the line.

An old woman was driving her blg, ____expensive____ car around a parking lot. She
                                          1
was looking for a parking space. Finally she _____ one. She was turning
                                                    2
into the space when a young man in a sports car drove in _____ of her. He
                                                                3
pulled into the space, got out of his car, and smiled at the woman. "_____,"
                                                                              4
he said. "But that's what you can do when you're _____ and fast."
                                                        5
The old woman crashed into the sports car. Then she put her car into

_____, backed up, and crashed into it again. The young man ran to the
        6
woman. "What are you doing?" he _____.
                                        7
The old woman _____ him her insurance card and smiled. "That's what
                      8
you can do when you're old and rich," she _____.
                                                9

B. Complete the sentences. Write your answer on the line. Check your answers in the
   Answer Key. Then sit with a partner. Student A asks the question; student B
   answers.

1. **A.** The old woman was driving her car around a building, right?

   B. No, she was driving her car around a _____ parking lot _____.

2. **A.** She was looking for a friend, right?

   B. No, she was looking for a _____.

3. **A.** A young man in a truck drove in front of her, right?

   B. No, a young man in a _____.

4. **A.** He pulled into the space, got out of his car, and yelled at the woman, right?

   B. No, he pulled into the space, got out of his car, and _____.

5. **A.** He said, "That's what you can do when you're young and smart," right?

   B. No, he said, "That's what you can do when you're young and _____."

6. **A.** The old woman backed into the sports car, right?

   B. No, she _____.

7. **A.** She gave the young man her credit card, right?

   B. No, she gave him her _____.

8. **A.** She said, "That's what you can do when you're old and fast," right?

   B. No, she said, "That's what you can do when you're old and _____."

4 LISTENING AND WRITING

☊ **Cover the sentences below with a piece of paper. You will hear the sentences. As you listen, write them on the lines. Then lift your paper and check your writing.**

1. An old woman was driving a big, expensive car.

2. She was turning into a parking space.

3. A young man was driving a sports car.

4. He took the woman's parking space.

5. He said he could do that because he was young and fast.

6. The old woman crashed her car into the sports car.

7. She gave the young man her insurance card.

8. She said she could do that because she was old and rich.

1. _____

2. _____

3. _____

4. _____

5. _____

6. _____

7. _____

8. _____

❺ RETELLING THE STORY

A. Write the story in your own words on the lines. Use the keywords to help you.

- old woman, drive, big expensive car, parking lot
- look, parking space
- find, one
- turn, space, young man, sports car, drive, in front of
- pull into, get out, smile
- sorry, what you can do, young, fast
- old woman, crash, sports car
- put reverse, back up, crash again
- young man, run, woman
- what, do, yell
- old woman, give, insurance card
- what you can do, old, rich

_____

_____

_____

_____

_____

_____

_____

_____

_____

_____

_____

_____

_____

_____

_____

_____

B. Tell the story to a partner. Use the pictures on the LISTENING TO THE STORY page to help you.

⑥ TALKING ABOUT THE TOPIC

What's Good about Being Old?

The young man said, "That's what you can do when you're young and fast." The old woman said, "That's what you can do when you're old and rich." What is good about being young? What is good about being old?

Find two ways to complete each sentence. Write your answer on the line. Then share your answers with the class.

When you're young, it's good because . . .

- _____.
- _____.

(For example: When you're young, it's good because you have your parents to help you.)

When you're old, it's good because . . .

- _____.
- _____.

(For example: When you're old, it's good because you have more free time.)

UNIT 14
Two Wishes

❶ BEFORE LISTENING

A. Complete the sentences with the words below. Write your answer on the line.

cruise   wish   first-class   appears   free

1. If something ___appears___, you can see it.

2. If you _____ a man from prison, you open the prison door and let

   him go.

3. If you make a _____, you want something good to happen.

4. If you are on a _____, you are traveling by ship.

5. If you have a _____ plane ticket, you paid a lot of money to ride in

   the front of the plane.

**B. You are going to hear a story about a genie. Look at the picture of the genie.
What is a genie? What can it do? If you know, tell the class.**

🎧 Look at the pictures as you listen to the story.

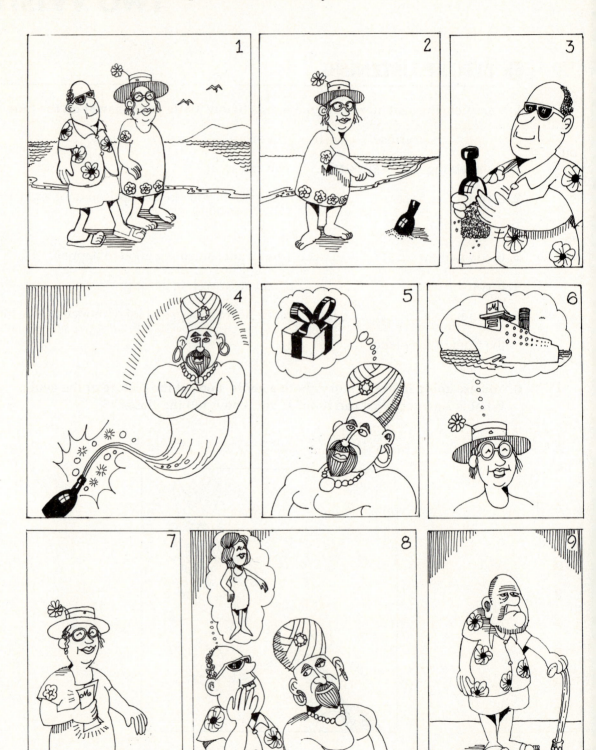

❸ CHECKING YOUR UNDERSTANDING

🎧 **A. Listen to the story again. As you listen, write the missing word on the line.**

A couple about _____*sixty*_____ years old was walking along the beach. The
₁
wife saw an old, dirty bottle on the _____. The husband picked up the
₂
bottle and _____ it with his hand. Suddenly a genie appeared.
₃
"_____ you for freeing me from the bottle," the genie said. "I want to give
₄
you a thank-you _____. You each have one wish. I will give you
₅
_____ you want."
₆

The wife said, "I want to _____ a trip around the world. Please send
₇
me and my _____ on a cruise."
₈

Poof! Suddenly the woman was holding two first-class _____ on the
₉
best ship in the world.

The husband looked at his wife and then _____ to the genie, "I want a
₁₀
wife who is thirty years younger than I am."

Poof! Suddenly the man was ninety _____ old.
₁₁

**B. Complete the sentences. Write your answer on the line. Check your answers in the
Answer Key. Then sit with a partner. Student A asks the question; student B
answers.**

1. **A.** The couple found an old photo on the beach, right?

    B. No, they found an old _____*bottle on the beach*_____.

2. **A.** The husband threw the bottle away, right?

    B. No, he _____.

3. **A.** Suddenly a woman appeared, right?

    B. No, suddenly a _____.

4. **A.** The genie wanted to give the couple a good-bye gift, right?

    B. No, the genie wanted to give them a _____.

5. **A.** The wife wanted to take a trip to Mexico, right?

    B. No, she wanted to take a trip _____.

6. **A.** The genie gave her two tickets on the best airplane in the world, right?

   B. No, the genie gave her two tickets on the best _____.

7. **A.** The man wanted a wife who was two years younger than he was, right?

   B. No, he wanted a wife who was _____.

8. **A.** Suddenly the man was thirty years old, right?

   B. No, suddenly he was _____.

4 LISTENING AND WRITING

Cover the sentences below with a piece of paper. You will hear the sentences. As you listen, write them on the lines. Then lift your paper and check your writing.

1. A couple found a bottle.

2. A genie came out of the bottle.

3. The genie gave the couple two wishes.

4. The wife wanted a trip around the world.

5. The genie gave her two tickets on a ship.

6. The man wanted a young wife.

7. He didn't get a young wife.

8. Suddenly he was ninety years old.

1. _____

2. _____

3. _____

4. _____

5. _____

6. _____

7. _____

8. _____

⑤ RETELLING THE STORY

A. Write the story in your own words on the lines. Use the keywords to help you.

- couple, sixty years old, beach
- wife, see, old, dirty bottle, sand
- husband, pick up, clean
- genie, appear
- genie, say, thank you, free, bottle
- to give, thank-you gift
- each, one wish
- wife, trip around the world
- please, send, cruise
- suddenly, hold, two tickets, ship
- man, look, wife, whisper, want, wife, thirty years younger
- suddenly, man, ninety years old

_____

_____

_____

_____

_____

_____

_____

_____

_____

_____

_____

_____

_____

_____

_____

B. Tell the story to a partner. Use the pictures on the LISTENING TO THE STORY page to help you.

⑥ TALKING ABOUT THE TOPIC

Should a Husband Be Older Than His Wife?

The man in the story wanted a wife who was thirty years younger than he was. Is it best when the husband is older than his wife? Or is it best when the wife is older than her husband? Or is it best when the husband and wife are the same age? What do you think?

A. Check (✓) your opinion and complete the sentence. (Check only one sentence.) Then share your answer with the class.

❑ It is best if the husband is older than his wife because _____

_____.

❑ It is best if the wife is older than her husband because _____

_____.

❑ It is best if the husband and wife are the same age because _____

_____.

B. In your country, is the husband usually older than his wife, or is the wife usually older than her husband? Tell the class.

C. Imagine this: A genie gives you one wish. You can have anything you want. What will you wish for? Tell the class.

The Bullies

❶ BEFORE LISTENING

A. Look at the photo. Describe what you see.

B. You are going to hear a story about a man who stopped at a restaurant for dinner. Look at the picture. What happened at the restaurant?

❷ LISTENING TO THE STORY

🎧 Look at the pictures as you listen to the story.

❸ CHECKING YOUR UNDERSTANDING

🎧 **A. Listen to the story again. As you listen, write the missing word on the line.**

Late at night, a truck _____*driver*_____ stopped at a restaurant. He parked his
1
truck, went into the restaurant, and _____ something to eat.
2
The truck driver was eating his _____ when two men on motorcycles
3
stopped at the restaurant. They _____ their motorcycles, walked into the
4
restaurant, and saw the truck driver. They walked over to him. One man poured
_____ on the truck driver's dinner. The other man poured water on his
5
_____. They wanted to fight with the truck driver. Why? They were bullies.
6
They liked to _____.
7
The truck driver didn't say anything. He stood up, _____ for his dinner,
8
and left the restaurant.
The two men laughed. "He isn't a very good _____, is he?" they said.
9
The waitress was looking out the _____. "No," she said, "and he isn't a
10
very good driver, either. He just drove his truck _____ two motorcycles."
11

**B. Answer the questions. Write your answer on the line. Check your answers in the
Answer Key. Then sit with a partner. Student A reads the question; student B
answers.**

1. **A.** Where did the truck driver stop?

   B. <u>He stopped at a restaurant.</u>

2. **A.** Who came into the restaurant?

   B. _____

3. **A.** What did one man pour on the truck driver's dinner?

   B. _____

4. **A.** What did the other man pour on the truck driver's head?

   B. _____

5. **A.** Why did the men want to fight the truck driver?

   B. _____

6. **A.** What did the truck driver say?

    B. _____.

7. **A.** What did the truck driver do?

    B. _____.

❹ LISTENING AND WRITING

🎧 **Cover the sentences below with a piece of paper. You will hear the sentences. As you listen, write them on the lines. Then lift your paper and check your writing.**

1. A truck driver was eating dinner at a restaurant.

2. Two men on motorcycles stopped at the restaurant.

3. They poured salt on the truck driver's dinner.

4. They poured water on his head.

5. The two men were bullies.

6. They wanted to fight.

7. The truck driver didn't say anything.

8. He walked out of the restaurant.

9. Then he drove his truck over the motorcycles.

1. _____

2. _____

3. _____

4. _____

5. _____

6. _____

7. _____

8. _____

9. _____

⑤ RETELLING THE STORY

A. Write the story in your own words on the lines. Use the keywords to help you.

- truck driver, stop, restaurant
- park, truck, go, restaurant, order
- two men, motorcycles, stop
- park, walk, see, truck driver
- pour, salt, dinner
- pour, water, head
- want, fight
- bullies

- say anything
- stand up, pay, leave
- laugh
- not, good fighter
- waitress, look, window
- not, good driver
- drive, truck, motorcycles

_____

_____

_____

_____

_____

_____

_____

_____

_____

_____

_____

_____

_____

_____

_____

B. Tell the story to a partner. Use the pictures on the LISTENING TO THE STORY page to help you.

❻ TALKING ABOUT THE TOPIC

What Should You Do about a Bully?

Read the pairs of ideas below.[1] Which idea is better? Check (✓) your answer and complete the sentence. Write your answer on the line. Then talk about your answers with the class.

1. ❑ Walk away from a bully   OR   ❑ Don't walk away from a bully

   because _____.

2. ❑ Fight a bully   OR   ❑ Don't fight a bully

   because _____.

3. ❑ Give the bully what the bully   OR   ❑ Don't give the bully what the
      wants (your hat, for example)   bully wants

   because _____.

4. ❑ Show your feelings (cry or   OR   ❑ Don't show your feelings
      get angry, for example)

   because _____.

5. ❑ Tell someone (a police officer   OR   ❑ Don't tell anyone about the
      or teacher, for example) about   bully
      the bully

   because _____.

---

[1]These ideas are from the Web site of the Canadian Red Cross. More ideas from the Red Cross are in the Answer Key.

UNIT 16
A Big Chicken

① BEFORE LISTENING

A. Look at the photo below. It is a photo of a butcher shop. Which things are usually at a butcher shop? Circle five words. (The first one is done for you.)

(meat)

apples

butcher

chicken

doctor

rice

scale

knives

teacups

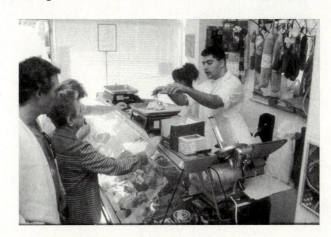

B. You are going to hear a story about a woman who is having a party at her house. Look at the drawing. What does the woman want to cook for the party?

❷ LISTENING TO THE STORY

🎧 Look at the pictures as you listen to the story.

❸ CHECKING YOUR UNDERSTANDING

🎧 **A. Listen to the story again. As you listen, complete the sentences. Circle the letter of your answer.**

1. A woman wanted to cook a
   a. chicken.
   b. lamb.

2. She went to a
   a. butcher shop.
   b. supermarket.

3. She wanted a
   a. big chicken.
   b. small chicken.

4. The butcher went to the
   a. front of the shop.
   b. back of the shop.

5. The woman said, "That chicken is too
   a. small."
   b. big."

6. The butcher had only
   a. two chickens.
   b. one chicken.

7. He came back with
   a. a different chicken.
   b. the same chicken.

8. He put his thumb on the
   a. scale.
   b. chicken.

9. The woman said, "I'll take
   a. both chickens."
   b. the second chicken."

B. Write the missing word on the line. Check your answers in the Answer Key. Then sit with a partner and read the conversation aloud. Student A begins.

A	B
1. Next?	I'd like a ___chicken___.
2. Just a minute—I'll get one from the _____ of the store.	A big one, please.
3. There! A nice, big chicken!	I think it's too small. Do you have a _____ one?
4. Yes. Just a minute. I'll get it.	A *really* big one, please.
5. There! Here's a bigger chicken!	That's better. But it's a little small, too.
	I'll take _____ chickens.

4 LISTENING AND WRITING

🎧 **Cover the sentences below with a piece of paper. You will hear the sentences. As you listen, write them on the lines. Then lift your paper and check your writing.**

1. A woman wanted to cook a chicken.

2. She asked the butcher for a big chicken.

3. The butcher showed her a chicken.

4. She asked for a bigger one.

5. The butcher had only one chicken.

6. He showed her the same chicken.

7. He said it was bigger.

8. The woman wanted to buy both chickens.

1. _____

2. _____

3. _____

4. _____

5. _____

6. _____

7. _____

8. _____

⑤ RETELLING THE STORY

A. Write the story in your own words on the lines. Use the keywords to help you.

- woman, cook, chicken, party
- go, butcher shop
- need, big chicken
- butcher, go, back, shop
- come back, chicken
- put, scale
- too small, bigger

- problem
- have, one chicken
- go, back, store
- come back, same chicken
- put, scale
- put, thumb, scale, push down
- woman, take, both

_____

_____

_____

_____

_____

_____

_____

_____

_____

_____

_____

_____

_____

_____

B. Tell the story to a partner. Use the pictures on the LISTENING TO THE STORY page to help you.

➏ TALKING ABOUT THE TOPIC

What Do Dishonest Businesspeople Do?

Think about ways businesspeople in your country try to cheat their customers. For example:

- *People sell packages of strawberries. Really nice strawberries are on the top of the package, but small, bad strawberries are on the bottom.*

- *Stores advertise that everything is 75 percent off. So people think that's a good deal. However, the stores raise the prices and then take 75 percent off. So the sale prices are the regular prices.*

Now write your examples on the lines below. Then share them with the class.

- _____
  _____

- _____
  _____

UNIT 17

The Vacation in Mexico

❶ BEFORE LISTENING

A. Answer the questions. Write the letter of your answer on the line.

1. How long does it take to fly from

   London to New York? ___*a*___

2. How long does it take to cook rice? _____

3. How long does it take the earth

   to go around the sun? _____

    a. It takes about six hours.

    b. It takes about twenty minutes.

    c. It takes about 365 days.

When do you use the expression "it takes . . ."? Talk about the expression with the class. Then write two sentences beginning with "It takes" or "It took."
For example:

- It takes fifteen minutes to walk to school.
- Yesterday it took me four hours to clean my house.

Now write your sentences and share them with the class.

- _____

- _____

B. You are going to hear a story about a man from New York who went on a vacation to Mexico. Look at the picture. What did the man see there?

🎧 Look at the pictures as you listen to the story.

❸ CHECKING YOUR UNDERSTANDING

🎧 **A. Listen to the story again. As you listen, read the story below. There are seven mistakes in the story. Cross out the mistakes. (The first one is done for you.)**

A New Yorker went on a vacation to ~~Jamaica~~. He hired a Mexican tour guide. First the tour guide took the New Yorker to a big park. The New Yorker said, "It's beautiful. How long did it take to build it?"

"About five months," said the tour guide.

"Five years?" said the New Yorker. "In the United States we can build a church in one year!"

Then the tour guide took the New Yorker to a famous theater. The New Yorker said, "It's beautiful. How long did it take to build it?"

"About ten years," said the tour guide.

"Five years?" said the New Yorker. "In the United States we can build a museum in one year!"

The Mexican tour guide was angry. She took the New Yorker on a long train ride. The New Yorker looked out his window. He saw the great pyramids in Mexico.

"Wow!" said the New Yorker. "Look at those mountains!"

The tour guide looked out the window. "Oh, my gosh!" she said. "I don't believe it. Yesterday they weren't there!"

B. Write the missing word on the line. Check your answers in the Answer Key. Then sit with a partner and read the conversation aloud. Student A begins.

A	B
1. This is one of Mexico's biggest churches.	It's beautiful. How long did it take to _____build_____ it?
2. About five years.	Five years? In the _____ _____ we can build a church in one year.

Unit 17 **99**

3. This is one of Mexico's most _____ museums.

It's beautiful. How long did it take to build it?

4. _____ five years.

Five years? In the United States we can build a museum in one year.

5. Next we'll go _____ a long bus ride.

Where are we going?

6. You'll see.

Wow! Look at those _____!

7. Oh, my gosh! _____ they weren't there!

④ LISTENING AND WRITING

Cover the sentences below with a piece of paper. You will hear the sentences. As you listen, write them on the lines. Then lift your paper and check your writing.

1. A New Yorker went to Mexico.

2. He hired a Mexican tour guide.

3. She took him to a church and to a museum.

4. He asked how long it had taken to build them.

5. He said they could build them faster in the United States.

6. The tour guide was angry.

7. She took the New Yorker to the pyramids.

8. He thought the pyramids were wonderful.

9. She said they hadn't been there the day before.

1. _____

2. _____

3. _____

4. _____

5. _____

6. _____

7. _____

8. _____

9. _____

⑤ RETELLING THE STORY

A. Write the story in your own words on the lines. Use the keywords to help you.

- New Yorker, go, vacation, Mexico
- hire, Mexican tour guide
- take, New Yorker, church
- beautiful, how long, take, build
- five years
- United States, build, one year
- take, New Yorker, museum
- beautiful, how long, take, build

- five years
- United States, build, one year
- angry, take, New Yorker, bus ride
- see, pyramids
- look out, window, see, pyramids
- wow, look
- yesterday, there

_____

_____

_____

_____

_____

_____

_____

_____

_____

_____

_____

_____

_____

B. Tell the story to a partner. Use the pictures on the LISTENING TO THE STORY page to help you.

❻ TALKING ABOUT THE TOPIC

What Are Popular Places to Visit in Your Country?

Imagine that a New Yorker is going to visit your country. You will be the New Yorker's tour guide.

Draw a map of your country. Put four places you will visit on the map. Number each place. Then, under the map, write a short description of each place. For example:

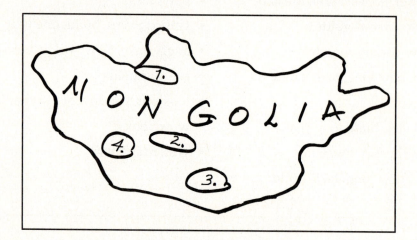

1. Lake Hovsgol is here. It is a clean, beautiful lake.
2. There are volcano craters here. There are beautiful views at the top of the craters.
3. This is the Gobi desert. It i hot, but there is ice that never melts.
4. There are beautiful waterfalls here.

Now draw your map on your own paper. Number four places. Write your descriptions on the lines below. Show your map to the class. Tell the class about each place on the map.

1. _____

_____

2. _____

_____

3. _____

_____

4. _____

_____

Four Parachutes

❶ BEFORE LISTENING

A. Complete the sentences with the words below. Write your answer on the line.

passengers   impossible   all of a sudden   pilot
backpacks   professor   parachute

1. The person who flies an airplane is the _____pilot_____.

2. The people who travel in an airplane are the _____.

3. A teacher who works at a university is a _____.

4. Something that happens fast and is a surprise happens _____.

5. Someone who jumps out of an airplane needs a _____.

6. The word that is the opposite of "possible" is _____.

7. Students who carry their books on their backs use _____.

B. You are going to hear a story about some people who were flying in an airplane. Look at the picture. What happened to the plane?

❷ LISTENING TO THE STORY

🎧 Look at the pictures as you listen to the story.

❸ CHECKING YOUR UNDERSTANDING

🎧 **A. Listen to the story again. As you listen, complete the sentences. Circle the letter of your answer.**

1. There were
   a. four passengers. *(circled)*
   b. two passengers.

2. One of the passengers was a
   a. student.
   b. mechanic.

3. There were only
   a. three parachutes.
   b. four parachutes.

4. The president of the United States said he was
   a. rich.
   b. important.

5. The university professor said he was
   a. intelligent.
   b. afraid.

6. The old man said he was ready to
   a. fly the airplane.
   b. die.

7. The student said there were
   a. two parachutes left.
   b. five parachutes left.

8. The professor jumped with the student's
   a. books.
   b. backpack.

B. Answer the questions. Write your answer on the line. Check your answers in the Answer Key. Then sit with a partner. Student A reads the question aloud; student B answers.

1. **A.** Who were the passengers?

   B. *They were the president of the United States, a university professor, an old man, and a student.*

2. **A.** What happened to the airplane?

   B. _____ .

3. **A.** How many parachutes were there?

   B. _____ .

4. **A.** What did the pilot, the president, and the professor do?

   B. _____ .

5. **A.** What did the old man say to the student?

   B. _____ .

6. **A.** What did the student say?

   B. _____ .

7. **A.** Why were there still two parachutes left?

   B. _____ .

④ LISTENING AND WRITING

Cover the sentences below with a piece of paper. You will hear the sentences. As you listen, write them on the lines. Then lift your paper and check your writing.

1. A pilot and four passengers were in an airplane.

2. The passengers were the president of the United States, a university professor, an old man, and a student.

3. The plane began to fall.

4. There were only four parachutes.

5. The pilot, the president, and the professor jumped out of the airplane.

6. There were still two parachutes left.

7. The professor jumped with the student's backpack.

1. _____

2. _____

3. _____

4. _____

5. _____

6. _____

7. _____

❺ RETELLING THE STORY

A. Write the story in your own words on the lines. Use the keywords to help you.

- pilot, four passengers, fly, airplane
- president, university professor, old man, student
- plane, fall
- sorry, four parachutes
- pilot, take, parachute, jump
- president, most important
- take, parachute, jump
- professor, most intelligent
- take, parachute, jump
- old man, take parachute
- ready, die
- two parachutes, left
- most intelligent, man, jump, backpack

_____

_____

_____

_____

_____

_____

_____

_____

_____

_____

_____

_____

_____

_____

_____

B. Tell the story to a partner. Use the pictures on the LISTENING TO THE STORY page to help you.

❻ TALKING ABOUT THE TOPIC

How Powerful Is the President of the United States?

In the story, the president of the United States said, "I am the most important man in the country." How important is the president of the United States?

Do you agree with this statement?

The president of the United States is the most powerful person in the world.

If you agree, put an X on the line near YES. If you do not agree, put an X on the line near NO. If your opinion is somewhere between YES and NO, put an X on the line between YES and NO. Explain your answer to the class.

YES--NO

Jokes

The Birthday Present

A rich woman was thinking about her mother. It was her mother's birthday, and she wanted to send her mother a nice birthday present.

The woman went to a pet shop. She saw a beautiful bird. The bird could sing, and it could speak seven languages. It cost fifty thousand dollars. The woman bought the bird and sent it to her mother.

The next day the woman called her mother on the telephone. "Mama," asked the woman, "How do you like the bird?"

"I'm eating it right now," her mother said. "It's delicious."

UNIT 2
The Skydiver

A young man wanted to try an exciting sport. He decided to try skydiving. So he went to a store and bought a parachute.

"I'm going to try skydiving!" he told his friends.

His friends were worried. "Skydiving is dangerous," they said. "What will you do if your parachute doesn't open?"

"If my parachute doesn't open," the young man said, "I'll take it back to the store and ask for my money back."

UNIT 3
The Memory Problem

A woman had a memory problem. So she went to a doctor.

"Doctor," the woman said. "I have a memory problem. I park my car somewhere, and I can't find it. I put my glasses somewhere, and I can't find them. I put my baby somewhere, and I can't find him."

"Hmmm," the doctor said. "This *is* serious. Tell me more about your problem."

"Problem?" the woman said. "What problem?"

UNIT 4
The Test

A student got a zero on a test. "Why did you give me a zero?" he asked the teacher. "Most of my answers are correct."

"Yes, but you copied Mary's answers," the teacher said.

"That's true," the student said. "How did you know?"

"Well," said the teacher, "your answers and Mary's answers are the same. Only answer number seven is different. Mary wrote, 'I don't know,' and you wrote, 'I don't know either.'"

UNIT 5
You've Changed

Mr. Mix was walking down the street when he met another man. "Mr. Peterson!" said Mr. Mix. "You've changed! You look very different. You used to be heavy, and now you're thin. You used to have black hair, and now you have gray hair. You used to wear glasses, and now you don't."

"I'm not Mr. Peterson," said the man. "I'm Mr. Jones."

"Wow!" said Mr. Mix. "You've changed your name too!"

UNIT 6
The New Job

A man came home and ran into the house. "I've found a great job!" he told his wife. "The hours are from eight in the morning to five o'clock in the afternoon. There are two coffee breaks, one in the morning and one in the afternoon. There's a one-hour lunch break. The pay is excellent. There's free health insurance. There's a three-week vacation too. What do you think?"

"It sounds great!" his wife said. "I'm very, very happy."

"Good!" the man said. "You start tomorrow."

UNIT 7
At the Barbershop

Dan was at a barbershop. He was getting a manicure and a shave. A young woman was giving him a manicure, and a young man was shaving him.

Dan liked the young woman. He decided to ask her for a date.

"Are you free for dinner tonight?" he asked her.

"I'm sorry. I can't have dinner with you," the woman answered. "I have a boyfriend."

"You can have dinner with me," Dan said. "Call your boyfriend. Tell him you're having dinner with a girlfriend."

"You tell him," the woman said. "He's shaving you."

UNIT 8
Two Ships in the Night

Late at night, a big ship was going through the water. The captain saw a light ahead. "It's a boat," he thought.

He picked up the radio. "Move to your right," he said.

The answer came back: "No, *you* move to *your* right."

The captain picked up the radio again. "Move to your right!" he said.

The answer came back: "No, *you* move to *your* right!"

The captain picked up the radio again. "Move to your right!" he shouted. "This is a big ship!"

The answer came back: "Yes, you are a big ship. And this is a big lighthouse."

UNIT 9
The Loan

Two friends, Sam and Mike, were riding on a bus. Suddenly, the bus stopped and bandits got on. The bandits began robbing the passengers. They were taking the passengers' jewelry and watches. They were taking all their money, too.

Sam opened his wallet and took out twenty dollars. He gave the twenty dollars to Mike.

"Why are you giving me this money?" Mike asked.

"Last week I didn't have any money, and you loaned me twenty dollars, remember?" Sam said.

"Yes, I remember," Mike said.

"I'm paying you back," Sam said.

UNIT 10
The Long and Happy Marriage

It was a special day for an old couple. It was their fiftieth wedding anniversary. They were very happy together.

A newspaper reporter went to their house. He wanted to write a story about them.

"Tell me," the reporter said. "What is the secret of your long and happy marriage?"

The old man answered. "Twice a week, we go to a romantic restaurant," he said. "First, we take a long walk to the restaurant. Then we have a delicious dinner. After dinner, we drink coffee and listen to the music. Then we take a long walk home. She goes on Tuesdays, and I go on Fridays."

UNIT 11
The Mean Boss

There was a mean boss in a factory. The boss liked to watch the workers. He wanted the workers to work hard.

One morning the boss came to the factory at nine o'clock. A man was drinking coffee. The boss came back at 9:30. The man was still drinking coffee. The boss was angry. "How much do you make a week?" he asked the man.

"Seven hundred dollars," the man said.

The boss gave the man seven hundred dollars. "Take the money and get out of here," he said.

Then the boss asked another worker, "What was that man's job?"

"He doesn't work here," the worker said. "He came to pick up a package."

UNIT 12
Dear John

A young soldier was far away from home. One day he got a letter from his girlfriend. The letter said:

Dear John,

I am sorry, but I have new boyfriend.

You have a very nice picture of me. Please send it back. I want to give it to my new boyfriend.

Maria

The soldier was angry. He asked his friends for pictures of women–aunts, sisters, girlfriends, mothers, or cousins. He put the pictures of the women in a big box, and he sent the box to his girlfriend. In the box he also put a letter. The letter said:

Dear Maria,

Please take your picture. I can't remember which one you are.

John

UNIT 13
The Parking Space

An old woman was driving her big, expensive car around a parking lot. She was looking for a parking space. Finally she found one. She was turning into the space when a young man in a sports car drove in front of her. He pulled into the space, got out of his car, and smiled at the woman. "Sorry," he said. "But that's what you can do when you're young and fast."

The old woman crashed into the sports car. Then she put her car into reverse, backed up, and crashed into it again. The young man ran to the woman. "What are you doing?" he yelled.

The old woman gave him her insurance card and smiled. "That's what you can do when you're old and rich," she said.

UNIT 14
Two Wishes

A couple about sixty years old was walking along the beach. The wife saw an old, dirty bottle on the sand. The husband picked up the bottle and cleaned it with his hand. Suddenly a genie appeared. "Thank you for freeing me from the bottle," the genie said. "I want to give you a thank-you gift. You each have one wish. I will give you anything you want."

The wife said, "I want to take a trip around the world. Please send me and my husband on a cruise."

Poof! Suddenly the woman was holding two first-class tickets on the best ship in the world.

The husband looked at his wife and then whispered to the genie, "I want a wife who is thirty years younger than I am."

Poof! Suddenly the man was ninety years old.

UNIT 15
The Bullies

Late at night, a truck driver stopped at a restaurant. He parked his truck, went into the restaurant, and ordered something to eat.

The truck driver was eating his dinner when two men on motorcycles stopped at the restaurant. They parked their motorcycles, walked into the restaurant, and saw the truck driver. They walked over to him. One man poured salt on the truck driver's dinner. The other man poured water on his head. They wanted to fight with the truck driver. Why? They were bullies. They liked to fight.

The truck driver didn't say anything. He stood up, paid for his dinner, and left the restaurant.

The two men laughed. "He isn't a very good fighter, is he?" they said.

The waitress was looking out the window. "No," she said, "and he isn't a very good driver, either. He just drove his truck over two motorcycles."

UNIT 16
A Big Chicken

A woman wanted to cook a chicken for a family party. So she went to a butcher shop.

"I need a big chicken," she told the butcher.

The butcher went to the back of the shop and came back with a chicken. He put it on the scale. "There!" he said. "A nice, big chicken!"

"I think it's too small," the woman said. "Do you have a bigger one?"

This was a problem for the butcher. He had only one chicken. He thought for a minute. Then he said, "Yes, I have a bigger chicken. I'll get it."

He took the chicken off the scale and carried it to the back of the store. Then he waited a minute and came back with the same chicken. He put it on the scale again. But this time he put his thumb on the scale and pushed down a little.

"There!" he said with a big smile. "Here's a bigger chicken!"

"That's better," the woman said. "But it's a little small, too. I'll take both chickens."

UNIT 17
The Vacation in Mexico

A New Yorker went on a vacation to Mexico. He hired a Mexican tour guide. First the tour guide took the New Yorker to a big church. The New Yorker said, "It's beautiful. How long did it take to build it?"

"About five years," said the tour guide.

"Five years?" said the New Yorker. "In the United States we can build a church in one year!"

Then the tour guide took the New Yorker to a famous museum. The New Yorker said, "It's beautiful. How long did it take to build it?"

"About five years," said the tour guide.

"Five years?" said the New Yorker. "In the United States we can build a museum in one year!"

The Mexican tour guide was angry. She took the New Yorker on a long bus ride. The New Yorker looked out his window. He saw the great pyramids in Mexico.

"Wow!" said the New Yorker. "Look at those pyramids!"

The tour guide looked out the window. "Oh, my gosh!" she said. "I don't believe it. Yesterday they weren't there!"

UNIT 18
Four Parachutes

A pilot and four passengers were flying in an airplane. The passengers were the president of the United States, a university professor, an old man, and a student. All of a sudden, the plane began to fall. The pilot said to the passengers, "I'm sorry, but there are only four parachutes for the five of us." Then the pilot took a parachute and jumped.

"I am the most important man in the country," said the president of the United States. "I must live!" He took a parachute and jumped.

"I am the most intelligent man in the country," said the university professor. "I must live!" He took a parachute and jumped.

The old man said to the student, "You take the last parachute, son. I am an old man, and I've had a good life. I'm ready to die."

"It's OK," said the student. "There are two parachutes left."

"That's impossible!" said the old man. "There were only four parachutes for the five of us."

"That's right," said the student. "But the most intelligent man in the country jumped out of the airplane with my backpack."

Answer Key

1. Before Listening (p.1)

A.
1. rich
2. pet
3. send
4. shop
5. languages
6. delicious

3. Checking Your Understanding (p. 3)

A.
1. thinking
2. send
3. pet
4. bird
5. seven
6. fifty
7. called
8. delicious

B.
1. present
2. bird
3. speak
4. thousand, send

UNIT 2

1. Before Listening (p. 7)

A. skydiving, exciting, dangerous, parachute, worried

3. Checking Your Understanding (pp. 9–10)

A.
1. a
2. b
3. b
4. a
5. a
6. b
7. a
8. b

B.
1. try
2. exciting
3. dangerous, parachute
4. open, back

UNIT 3

3. Checking Your Understanding (p. 15)

A. Mistakes: teacher, back, motorcycle, cat, write

B.
1. memory
2. park
3. glasses
4. find, somewhere
5. him
6. about

6. Talking about the Topic (p. 18)

B.

Memory Tips

1. Remembering Names

- When you meet someone new, say the person's name while the person is still standing in front of you. (For example, "Nice to meet you, Katherine.")
- When you meet someone new, try to associate the name with something. For example, if you meet a man named "Tyler," think of him tying his shoes. The next time you see him, you'll probably remember "tying his shoes." Then you'll remember the name "Tyler."
- Often we have trouble remembering people's names when they're in the wrong place—when we see classmates at the supermarket, for example. So think about about where, not who. Don't try to remember who the people are. Try to remember where you met them. If you think about where you know the people from, you can usually remember their names.

2. Remembering Where Something Is

- Put things in the same place every time. For example, keep your keys in a box near the door. Put them there every time you come into your house or apartment.
- Let's say you can't find your glasses. Think about the last time you wore them. Were you reading? Were you watching TV? Go back to the place and look there.
- Pay attention. For example, if you put some papers in a notebook, say to yourself, "I'm putting these papers in my red notebook." If you come out of a subway station in a new place, look around you. What buildings, signs, and streets do you see? As you walk away from the station, look back a few times. Say to yourself, for example, "There's a newspaper stand, a post office with two mailboxes in front of it . . ."

UNIT 4

1. Before Listening (p. 19)

A.
1. too
2. either
3. either
4. too
5. either

3. Checking Your Understanding (p. 21)

A.
1. test
2. zero
3. answers
4. copied
5. did
6. same
7. different
8. wrote

B.

2. gave
3. Most, answers
4. know, wrote

UNIT 5

1. Before Listening (p. 25)

B.

1. T
2. F
3. F
4. F
5. T

3. Checking Your Understanding (p. 27)

A.

1. street
2. changed
3. now
4. have
5. used
6. I'm
7. too

B.

3. Mix
4. heavy
5. hair
6. wore
7. not
8. name

UNIT 6

3. Checking Your Understanding (pp. 33–34)

A.

1. a
2. b
3. b
4. b
5. a
6. b

B.

1. job
2. hours
3. there
4. afternoon, insurance
5. free
6. happy
7. tomorrow

UNIT 7

3. Checking Your Understanding (p. 39)

A.

1. barbershop
2. shave
3. woman
4. a date

5. dinner
6. can't
7. boyfriend
8. a girlfriend
9. shaving

B.

1. tonight, have
4. dinner, tell

UNIT 8

1. Before Listening (p. 43)

A. ship, water, captain, boat, radio

3. Checking Your Understanding (p. 45)

A.

1. water
2. light
3. up
4. right
5. again
6. answer
7. shouted
8. ship

B.

1. hear
3. right
4. move
5. big, lighthouse

UNIT 9

1. Before Listening (p. 49)

A.

1. bandits
2. rob
3. passengers
4. jewelry
5. wallets
6. loan

3. Checking Your Understanding (pp. 51–52)

A.

1. riding
2. got
3. watches
4. wallet
5. money
6. any
7. remember
8. back

B.

1. bus
2. bandits got on
3. robbing them
4. jewelry, watches, and money
5. twenty dollars
6. Mike
7. week you loaned me twenty dollars
8. paying you back

UNIT 10

1. Before Listening (p. 55)
A.
1. couple
2. wedding anniversary
3. reporter
4. secret
5. marriage
6. twice

3. Checking Your Understanding (pp. 57–58)
A.
1. an old
2. fiftieth
3. happy
4. newspaper
5. marriage
6. man
7. week
8. take a long walk
9. coffee
10. Fridays

B.
1. It was their fiftieth wedding anniversary.
2. A newspaper reporter went to their house.
3. He wanted to write a story about them.
4. He asked them, "What is the secret of your long and happy marriage?"
5. They go to a romantic restaurant.
6. They go twice a week.
7. They drink coffee and listen to the music.
8. He goes on Fridays, and she goes on Tuesdays.

UNIT 11

1. Before Listening (p. 61)
A.
1. e
2. a
3. b
4. d
5. c

3. Checking Your Understanding (pp. 63–64)
A.
1. boss
2. watch
3. o'clock
4. still
5. make
6. gave
7. out
8. job
9. doesn't
10. package

B.
1. mean
2. factory
3. coffee
4. angry
5. week

6. Seven hundred dollars
7. get out of here
8. pick up a package

UNIT 12

1. Before Listening (p. 67)
A.
1. b
2. c
3. a
4. d

3. Checking Your Understanding (pp. 69–70)
A. Mistakes: mother, Michael, happy, men, present, ring

B.
1. He was far away from home.
2. He got a letter from his girlfriend.
3. She wanted to give it to her new boyfriend.
4. He felt angry.
5. They gave him pictures of women.
6. He put them in a box.
7. He put a letter in the box.
8. It said, "Please take your picture. I can't remember which one you are."

6. Talking about the Topic (p. 72)
B. These are the most popular answers given by people in the United States:

1. a
Seventy-five percent of the people thought the best way to break up was in person. Women thought the second best way was on the phone; men said the second best way was in a letter. Some men said they liked to just disappear, but no women said that was a good idea.

2. b
People said that in their experience, women usually ended a romance, but the difference was small. Sixty percent of the people said the woman usually ended a romance, and forty percent said it was usually the man.

3. b
Ninety-five percent of the people said it is more difficult when someone breaks up with them.

4. a, b, and f
These were the top answers, although more women than men gave "f" as their answer.

UNIT 13

1. Before Listening (p. 73)
A. drive, parking lot, parking space, crash, sports car, reverse, back up, insurance

3. Checking Your Understanding (pp. 75–76)
A.
1. expensive
2. found
3. front
4. Sorry
5. young
6. reverse
7. yelled
8. gave
9. said

B.

1. parking lot
2. parking space
3. sports car drove in front of her
4. smiled at the woman
5. fast
6. crashed into the sports car
7. insurance card
8. rich

UNIT 14 _____

1. Before Listening (p. 79)

A.

1. appears
2. free
3. wish
4. cruise
5. first-class

B. A genie is a magical spirit that is often in Arabian stories. A genie sometimes lives in a bottle or lamp and has special powers. If you call a genie, it will do what you want.

3. Checking Your Understanding (pp. 81–82)

A.

1. sixty
2. sand
3. cleaned
4. Thank
5. gift
6. anything
7. take
8. husband
9. tickets
10. whispered
11. years

B.

1. bottle on the beach
2. cleaned it with his hand
3. genie appeared
4. thank-you gift
5. around the world
6. ship in the world
7. thirty years younger than he was
8. ninety years old

UNIT 15 _____

3. Checking Your Understanding (pp. 87–88)

A.

1. driver
2. ordered
3. dinner
4. parked
5. salt
6. head
7. fight
8. paid
9. fighter
10. window
11. over

B.

1. He stopped at a restaurant.
2. Two men came into the restaurant.
3. He poured salt on his dinner.
4. He poured water on his head.
5. They were bullies. They liked to fight.
6. He didn't say anything.
7. He drove his truck over the motorcycles.

6. Talking about the Topic (p. 90)

The Canadian Red Cross suggests these answers:

1. Walk away from a bully because bullies like a lot of attention from other people. If you just walk away, bullies don't get attention; there is nothing to watch.

2. Don't fight a bully because you will probably lose the fight. Bullies usually win fights because they almost always make trouble with people who are smaller than they are.

3. Try not to give the bully what the bully wants because the bully will keep taking things from you. If you give bullies your hat one day, for example, they might ask for money the next day. But if bullies have a knife or a gun, give them what they want.

4. Don't show your feelings because bullies like to make people cry or get angry. If it's difficult for you not to show your feelings, practice at home in front of the mirror.

5. Always tell someone about a bully because bullies often stop if a teacher or police officer knows what they are doing. If you tell someone, and that person doesn't help you, tell someone else.

(These answers are from the Web site of the Canadian Red Cross. They are good ideas for people who live in the United States or Canada.)

UNIT 16 _____

1. Before Listening (p. 91)

A. meat, butcher, chicken, scale, knives

3. Checking Your Understanding (p. 93)

A.

1. a
2. a
3. a
4. b
5. a
6. b
7. b
8. a
9. a

B.

1. chicken
2. back
3. bigger
5. both

UNIT 17 _____

1. Before Listening (p. 97)

A.
1. a
2. b
3. c

3. Checking Your Understanding (pp. 99–100)

A. Mistakes: Jamaica, park, months, theater, ten, train, mountains

B.
1. build
2. United States
3. famous
4. About
5. on
6. pyramids
7. Yesterday

UNIT 18 _____

1. Before Listening (p. 103)

A.
1. pilot
2. passengers
3. professor
4. all of a sudden
5. parachute
6. impossible
7. backpacks

3. Checking Your Understanding (pp. 105–106)

A.
1. a
2. a
3. b
4. b
5. a
6. b
7. a
8. b

B.
1. They were the president of the United States, a university professor, an old man, and a student.
2. It began to fall.
3. There were four parachutes.
4. They jumped out of the plane.
5. He said, "You take the last parachute, son. I am an old man, and I've had a good life. I'm ready to die."
6. He said, "It's OK. There are two parachutes left."
7. The professor jumped out of the airplane with the student's backpack.

CD Tracking Guide